SAUL'S ARMOR

Reforming Your Building and Organization for Ministry

BILL KEMP

DISCIPLESHIP RESOURCES

P O BOX 340003 • NASHVILLE, TN 37203-0003
w w w . d i s c i p l e s h i p r e s o u r c e s . o r g

Cover design by Christa Schoenbrodt.

ISBN 13: 978-0-88177-518-1

Library of Congress Cataloging-in-Publication Data on File.

Contents

Preface: A License to Change Everything

Remember when you first received your driver's license? I remember sitting solo behind the steering wheel and tasting freedom. The radio sang, "Go where you want to go, do what you want to do." Now leap forward and think of your worst car. I remember once owning a big blue Plymouth nine-seat station wagon which would stall three times each morning on the way to work—on the days that it actually started. Once I arrived, no parking space was big enough to parallel-park that car. On the other hand, I also remember the sporty little import we bought as new parents. We then took a nine-hundred-mile road trip to show off the baby (our son, not the car). I still have nightmares from the hours of trying to fit toys, suitcases, diaper bags, and a bassinette into a trunk the size of a breadbox. All of that goes with the driver's license.

Your congregation has a license to do ministry. Jesus said, "Go and make disciples of all nations (Matthew 28:19)." This liberating call sets us free to implement all the love and missionary zeal in the gospel. Our hearts sing, "Gates of hell can never 'gainst that church prevail," and as a part of the Body of Christ we move forward.

The vehicles you have for this mission are the buildings and committee structure of your church. Sometimes this vehicle will behave so beautifully that the people will have no difficulty doing their work of witness, nurture, and missional outreach. Major milestones in congregational growth and community service will whiz by your windows. Outsiders will marvel at how the people, buildings, and governing groups mesh together to get things done. Structures, while rooted in concrete and legislative process, can be engineered to fly like extensions of the Spirit's dove.

At other times, you may experience chaos and despair. Leaders will become discouraged on the long road between every new idea and its implementation. Committees will discuss trivial issues to death and leave vital matters tabled indefinitely. It will take a maximum effort to get the buildings to pass inspection, let alone appear comfortable and inviting to newcomers. Your congregation's structures will remind you of that sometime non-functioning car that you owned. Your aging facility, poor location, or bureaucratic committees may leave you stranded beside the high road to mission. You see other congregations—meeting in theaters, schools, and prefab buildings—attract religious seekers from your town's streets. Some within your congregation may move to other churches because of the building. Your congregation's buildings and policies may be negating your church's ministry. We expect more today from church than previous generations, and the post-Darwinian age favors only the fittest of organizational structures. We either function well or we dwindle and die.

Leo Tolstoy wrote, "All happy families resemble one another; each unhappy family is unhappy in its own way" (*Anna Karenina*). The same thought applies to congregations and their structures. When the buildings and the governing procedures of a church are right, a happy linkage occurs between the resources of a church and its work in the world. Form follows function in this type of church. These buildings and committees respond to congregational ministry and mission. Having the right organization and facilities enables such congregations to feel centered in worship and in theological tradition. Functional structures support our being as well as our doing. The church with a good vision-casting and decision-making process looks like an organization that belongs to Jesus Christ. It lovingly maintains its facilities without becoming idolatrously obsessive about them. When they are happy, Presbyterian churches look very much like Lutheran or United Methodist churches, and each polity achieves the same good things through differing means. Further, when the structures are right, a century-old traditional congregation can be as relevant and happily functional as the most "emerging church" fellowship.

Each congregation saddled with a dysfunctional structure, however, is unhappy in its own way. One church spends all of its resources heating and cooling an ark of a building that serves only a handful of people. Another is a "Historic Building" neatly imprisoned by a Civil War-era cemetery and an invisible plaque by the door that states, "Here, on this spot, nothing may ever happen again." Another congregation may have the perfect location for growth, but its board and committees resist change and remain deadlocked. Many churches in the United States today have some combination of structural issues. Their leaders feel isolated because no one else seems to deal with these problems. They think, "Why does the roof leak at the same time the secretary goes on maternity leave and the trustees are in a snit? Why is this happening to us (and only to us)?" Many church leaders fall into this pit of despair.

Cutting Through to Simplicity

In the face of what at first seems to be hopelessly complex situation, this book offers an overview that reduces the clutter to a few guiding principles. My goal is to write simply and clearly about what you need to know in order to change. I will present a transitional process for restructuring both physical and organizational entities. Further, I will demonstrate how facility change depends upon organizational change and how both lead to congregational growth.

To keep it as simple as possible, I have grouped the material around five essential areas, each with an easy to remember verb:

- Welcoming and Witnessing (Engage)
- Worship and Faith Development (Nurture)

- Training and Deployment (Equip)
- Implementing New Ideas (Envision)
- Money to Mission (Send)

These areas are like the five smooth stones that David carried to confront Goliath. Chapters two through six provide assessment tools for measuring the dysfunction inherent in each structure. If mastered, concepts like making our walls say welcome will provide strategy and tactics for making meaningful change. The five action-oriented verbs (Engage, Nurture, Equip, Envision, and Send) will enable you to group the structures of your church in a way that is strategic and missional, rather than traditional, maintenance-minded, institutional groupings, which tend to dilute intentionality and stifle creativity.

I have not provided a separate category for the facility. Each of the smooth stones presented has a material and a human component. Mind and matter must change simultaneously. Ineffective structures will continue to enslave us as long as we separate the physical aspects of the church building from the spiritual experience of the church. Part of the wrong thinking that keeps us from changing our ineffective structures is the tendency to treat the church's material assets as things unto themselves. For example, we ask people to serve on a committee that is solely charged with maintaining the building instead of incorporating the committee members into a team empowered to align the facilities of the church with its mission. We ask other people to serve on a finance committee because they are good with numbers or have demonstrated a knack for pinching pennies in their secular employment. We rarely ask our money managers to discern what God is doing in the community and to attempt to align the expenditures of the church so that we can partner more effectively with God.

By speaking about structures as vehicles for achieving these five important functions of the church, I propose a shift in how we think about our work. For example, those who serve on a committee overseeing the landscaping of the church need to contemplate how their decisions enhance or diminish the congregation's capacity to engage those who are not part of the church and welcome them into a new relationship with God. A simple matter for changed thinking: parking spaces and entrances need to be viewed in terms of their capacity to welcome visitors rather than as possessions of the current members. The same shift in thinking will help those assigned to worship committees or Christian education. Trustees are not simply responsible for maintaining a sanctuary, but for providing a great space for worship. Another task calls us to equip the leadership. Decisions about office equipment and clergy housing need to be viewed in the context of recruitment and deployment.

I use the word *envision* to talk about the structures that formulate and communicate the strategy and short-term goals of the church. The whole administrative structure in many churches needs coaching to move from thinking of the church building and location as the thing that gives the congregation its identity. If we identify ourselves as the people who belong to this particular building, then we will never act to change the building or move on when it fails to meet our purposes. A congregation may be accustomed to thinking of themselves as "the little brown church in the vale," but suburban sprawl now forces them to reformulate their congregational identity. How can this example adapt to the new reality?

Finally, money must always be linked to mission. The weekly offering is not the necessary evil that pays our bills; the offering is our joyful investment in the structures that demonstrate our love of God and God's love for others. In this way money spent locally and provides heat in the sanctuary is not viewed as different from money that goes to Tanzania and drills a new well for thirsty people. Both manifest the congregation's unique understanding of its missional calling. For this area in particular, as well as for the other four stones, church leaders must guard against participation in the mindset that separates the material from the spiritual. This idolatry, which honors the temple above God, the money above its mission, and a people's assets above their faith, always leads a congregation down a path that leads away from health, growth, and vitality. The final chapter of this book will help leaders name this idolatry in their own church and cultivate new sources of capital to make the structural changes they envision.

Chapters two through six are self-contained discussions that can be used separately for study. Each chapter begins with a self-test for determining the effectiveness of your existing structures as they relate to that area. A worksheet is provided at the end of the book so a church council or the leaders at a planning retreat can do all five tests and arrive at a transitional priority list. The chapters also end with exercises to help congregations reconnect their structures with their missional goals.

Remember David selecting stones at the brook? David would not have chosen those five smooth stones if he was not confident in the power of God and the blessing of agility that his shepherd lifestyle and developed in him.

You, the Leader and the Reader

I assume you are an active leader, either layperson or ordained, who loves the church and hopes to see your congregation fulfill its great commission to make disciples. I also assume that some area of your church's structure is currently letting you down. I write as a church consultant and transitional specialist located in a region where most church buildings are about one hundred years old. Many of these buildings have only had cosmetic changes over the years. Some added an educational wing in the 1950s, or converted the adjacent parsonage into youth rooms and office space. By and large, their concessions to a world that long ago forgot the Akron Plan of church design have been minimal. (The "Akron Plan" style of church design was popular around 1900 and featured curved auditorium style seating and a semicircular sanctuary with Sunday school classrooms opening into the sanctuary.) Everywhere I look I see aging church buildings that house declining congregations. I also see population shifts and growth and the opportunity for ministry.

As soon as we set out to change anything in our church facility, we are likely to encounter an organizational structure that prevents change from occurring. If the decision-making process in our church were rational and proactive, then the change we are now proposing would have happened long ago. It is my premise that organizational structures and physical structure are always intertwined. Reorganization around mission may lead a congregation to relocate entirely. It also may result in the leadership appreciating afresh the congregation's history in this particular place and lead them to reaffirm their commitment to their current neighborhood.

There is no right answer to the question, "How ought the church be organized?" Just as no single answer is correct concerning what a church building should look like or how it should be maintained. There are, however, many wrong answers. I pray that this book will help you find what is right for your mission and ministry today!

The Limits of Efficiency

A cartoon in the business section of the paper showed a Roman galley with a group of executives huddled around a table. Behind them were rows of empty benches and oars. One lone rower sat in the stern. The caption read, "I don't get it; after all the budget cuts to streamline the workforce, why aren't we moving faster?"

Many churches today are seeking to restructure their physical structures to gain efficiency. They can no longer afford to provide utilities and maintenance on rooms that are used only once a week, or to heat a high ceiling sanctuary for the handful of the faithful. Small churches merge or close. Larger congregations eagerly seek renters. Old churches apply for historic building status and historic preservation grants. Congregations with more progressive leadership seek to relocate to more efficient buildings on the edge of suburbia. All of these things may be appropriate in particular settings and essential for survival. The question that rarely gets asked, however, is, "Will we still feel good about ourselves after the dust settles?" Congregations should only make those structural changes that enhance their mission, reflect truthfully their vision, and resonate with their congregational identity.

The Three Hurdles

Think about the basic steps that need to occur for there to be significant change in any human endeavor. Whether we are talking about a million dollar building project or losing twenty pounds, three hurdles need clearance:

1. A shift in perspective happens so that the leadership becomes focused on mission. In the example of the dieter, this means seeking personal well-being rather than being content to maintain the status quo.

2. Transition from the old to the new happens. How we achieve the goal needs planning and communication. A system must be put in place for counting calories, collecting pledges, and approving contracts.

3. The sacrifices required for the vision to become reality need acknowledgement and acceptance. Church people are willing to make sacrifices when they understand the purpose for their sacrifice.

In drawing an analogy between structural change in the church and the complex world of weight control, I have entered sensitive territory. If losing weight were simply a matter of following the right diet regime or taking the right pill, very few of us would be obese. If changing the church's facility was just a matter of doing the appropriate capital funding campaign and hiring a reputable contractor, few of our congregations would be so inadequately housed. Structures, whether they are physical ones or the mental/organizational ones of our thought patterns and traditions, are intimately tied to our sense of identity. The role models for serious structural change in the church are few and the hurdles before the congregation that departs from the dysfunctional ways are many.

Loss and Change

Every significant change involves loss. Even when there is unanimous approval of some structural change, someone leaves the meeting with a sense of loss. Perhaps the feeling relates to the old nesting instinct. Church is, for most of us, home.

Nothing is as inevitable as change. With change comes loss, and with loss comes change. With this in mind, I would encourage any task force or church council seeking to bring about change to begin meetings by praying the Prayer of Saint Ignatius of Loyola:

> Teach us, Good Lord
> To serve you as you deserve.
> To give and not count the cost.
> To fight and not heed the wounds.
> To toil and not to seek for rest.
> To labor and not to ask for any reward
> Except that of knowing that we do Your Will.
> Through Jesus Christ our Lord, Amen.

CHAPTER ONE

Agility: A New Kind of Fit

*Then Saul dressed David in his own tunic. He put a coat
of armor on him and a bronze helmet on his head.
David fastened on his sword over the tunic and tried walking
around, because he was not used to them. "I cannot go in these,"
he said to Saul, "because I am not used to them." So he took
them off. Then he took his staff in his hand, chose five smooth stones
from the stream, put them in the pouch of his shepherd's bag and,
with his sling in his hand, approached the Philistine.*

I Samuel 17:38-40

Saul must have been surprised when David refused to wear his
armor. To wear the tunic and bronze helmet of the king should have
been a great honor for the boy. Saul's generosity seems almost as remarkable as David's honesty. David is blunt, "These things don't fit." David
may have initially rejected Saul's armor because of the way that it failed
to fit his body. Saul was known to be a head taller than anyone else, and
David was small when compared to his brothers. Saul's armor pieces did
not buckle to fit David. David, however, knew a deeper reason why the

armor did not fit. His methods differed radically from Saul's. The old tools of the warrior's trade were useless to David. Taking on the weight of the breastplate, helmet, and shield would both be burdensome and an offense to David's single minded dependence upon God. David operates under a new paradigm that excluded the old structures.

David's predicament went far beyond physical fit. His way of thinking challenged the motives, tactics, goals, and objectives of the Israeli military leadership. The old structures did not fit the spirit of transformation that God would unleash. In the same manner, your current physical and organizational structures may not fit the new identity, motivation, and future to which your congregation is being led.

David could have worn armor from a soldier closer to his own size. I imagine that David realized that doing so might then lead to practices and structures incompatible with the new identity of God's people. It would compromise core values of the faithful relationship with God. As we attempt to patch old structures so they can remain in service a few more years, we need an awareness of how our decisions support or repudiate our faith, values, and missional identity.

The relationship between structures and identity is a key concept to understand. You may have picked up this book because you sensed the need for a better fit between your congregation and its facilities. You may wish for help in developing a leaner committee structure. You might be saying, "If only we had more parking, a new addition, or a way to limit our board meetings to ninety minutes." This way of approaching "fit" relates to the first of the two aspect of David's dismissal of Saul's armor. It says, "I am still going to wear armor into battle, but it will be lighter and fit better." What if we approached "fit" as David did? How do these words of Jesus inform us: "No, new wine must be poured into new wineskins" (Luke 5:38)?

When David goes out to confront Goliath, we sense the type of church structures needed for ministry in the twenty-first century. As a shepherd, David protected sheep, which were often vulnerable in the night. David chose implements on the basis of efficiency rather than tradition. His shepherd's garb is flexible. Nothing hinders his movements.

He chooses five smooth stones, not for their beauty, but because they are the right weight and shape for the job. The sling, rather than sword, compliments David's agility and size. While Goliath is still laughing with surprise, David moves into range. His weapon fires before Goliath unsheathes his sword.

Human nature tends to improve an item by making it more complex. The simple helmet, shield, and breastplate of the late Roman era evolved into the full armor of the medieval knight. The well-equipped knight needed assistants to help him to his feet and a specially bred horse to carry him into battle. Even before the advent of gunpowder, this system fell prey to the crossbow and the agility of less resource-intensive battle techniques.

Why does today's church need to change the structures that have served us well in the past? As a United Methodist, I know my denomination better than other churches, but my comments in this paragraph can apply to the organizational structure of every denomination. Note that the organizational manual (*The Book of Discipline*) used in the United Methodist Church today is an accumulation and modification of a system of church order designed in the mid-1700s. In its day it enabled a very popular movement (Methodism was then the religion of the people) to mobilize its resources to do great acts of mission and evangelization. Its structure was based upon enlightenment principles that gave equal weight to scripture, reason, experience, and tradition. *The Discipline* now tops 750 pages, let alone the much longer supplemental *Book of Resolutions*. The tone of our church order is fixed in legal and governmental language rather than in the strategic tongue of today's competitive marketplace.

Let us recognize with honesty that our current organizational structures and buildings developed in a time when religion was a respected and integral part of human society. We live now in a different era. Organizational meetings in the local church fail to have quorums because they were designed in a time when people wanted to belong to committees. The bells in our steeples fail to invite people to worship because they are inaudible in today's mass media culture. Even if we were to double entry-level salaries, we would fail to attract the best and brightest young adults into full time Christian service because our structures fail to support their values. We find ourselves the beleaguered owners of high-rise, hierarchical, denominational structures in a time when the world is flat, as Thomas Friedman describes our global culture in *The World Is Flat: A Brief History of the Twenty-first Century* (Farrar, Straus, and Giroux, 2005)]

Two Levels of Fit

Today church leaders constantly need to evaluate church structures and change that which does not fit. These discussions will take place on two levels:

1. Level one considers fit in terms of efficiency, comfort, and convenience. We make decisions on this level every day and may think that these are the only criteria for making church decisions. I notice, for example that the department store has my favorite brand and style of jeans on sale. I quickly duck into the changing room to see if the size I had last time still fits. My decision to buy is based upon price (economics), past satisfaction (comfort), and proximity (this is the store I am in). Next time your church discuss a facility change, notice how little of the debate moves beyond these considerations of efficiency, comfort, and convenience.

2. Level two expects structure to fit in terms of values, identity, and missional strategy. Here we ask how our structures support the church as it seeks to transform the community. Do the proposed improvements express any of the core values of the congregation? Will they help us witness to our faith, nurture better disciples, cultivate strong leadership, or transform the community? These questions are more like what happens when I travel down the aisle at the department store and pick up a wild Hawaiian shirt and ask my wife, "Do you think it's me?" The fit I am looking for is one that goes beyond comfort and says something about my personality. I may want to

introduce others to "the new me" with that floral shirt. Our churches live in a society that has grown weary of the old institutional structures. To reconnect with our culture we need to do more than merely modernize our structures. We need to make them fit with our mission, our vision, and our sense of theological identity.

Elevating Thinking

One of the great tasks of leadership is to lift people from level one thinking to level two thinking. This is not to say that discussions about efficiency, comfort, and cost are unimportant. However, even the most mundane structural decision requires some level two considerations. Take, for example, the selection of a cover-stock for the weekly worship bulletin. What could be more obviously level one? We ask, "What works best with our equipment?" (efficiency), "Where did we buy them last time?" (convenience), and "How many should we order to get a price break?" (cost). Leaders in growing churches ask level two questions about the strangest things, from global ministry to accepted practices in the community. Think about how this comes into action in an everyday decision: I notice that when a church becomes serious about reaching a younger audience or becomes intentional about inviting unchurched people to worship, the church always changes the feel, color, and shape of the bulletin. The new bulletin shape is not likely to convince a young adult or a seeker to return; the altered format conveys some of the new self-identity that the congregation is adopting. Look at your church's current bulletin. Ask: "Does this reflect our understanding of mission? How does it describe our community of faith? Does it show how we want to be seen?" Nothing says stuck in the ninetieth century better than a Times-Roman type font on a neatly folded 8 $\frac{1}{2}$ by 11 page. Leaders in growing churches know that something doesn't fit simply because it is a three-year-old tradition or because it is cheap, but when it expresses our current vision, our identity, and our missional strategy.

Good leaders continually lift up strategic and value-oriented questions when discussing even the most basic matters. They are not obsessively detail oriented, but they understand how smaller things communicate the organization's message as well as the large plans. Good leaders help people to understand what matters in the church. They are driven to communicate at every turn the mission, vision, and identity of their congregation. Developing a decision-making process based upon commonly understood values and priorities is more important to them than being right on any one item. They are not afraid to over-communicate and overstate the long-term goals of the church, hoping always to reinforce these defining objectives.

Identity

The three key concepts of vision, mission, and identity are the force that lifts structural discussions from level one to level two. In previous books I have focused on restoring a congregation's sense of vision (*Ezekiel's Bones: Rekindling Your Congregation's Spiritual Passion*, Discipleship Resources) and mission (*Jonah's Whale: Reconnecting Your Congregation with its Mission*, Discipleship Resources). Congregational identity seems to have a peculiar relationship with functional structures. Self-image weighs heavily when we make decisions about buildings, staffing, and organizational structure. In fact, current needs, stated objectives, and carefully crafted mission statements often take a back seat when church leaders have a chance to set in concrete something that really makes a statement about who they perceive themselves to be.

- If a church identifies itself with its past achievements, then its leaders may be prone to patch together outdated equipment and fund staffing that no longer meets current needs.

- If a church identifies itself as a church that loves children, then this self-awareness will show up in a variety of structural choices. The worship services will maximize the involvement of youth and meet the needs of the children. They will make decisions about staffing and room renovation based on what is best for the children.

An especially painful example of identity trumping missional vision is the way congregations in my area have handled the issue of racial inclusion. In Pittsburgh, the weekly worship hour continues to be the most segregated segment of our society. We rely on many excuses for the lack of diversity in our churches and have also crafted some very fine statements against racism, but the key issue for Pittsburgh, as well as for most metropolitan regions, is one of identity. Until recently, whenever a congregation was started in a community, its structures were tailored to the meet needs of the people of a particular economic class or of an ethnic tradition within that neighborhood. Their identity as a fellowship became enmeshed with the culture and ethnicity of that founding membership. Over the years most neighborhoods change. Our society has become more diverse. Congregations founded before 1970 tend to react by identifying with their founders rather than with their current neighbors. If their neighborhood becomes largely Latino, they are more likely to rent space to an emerging congregation than start new Spanish language worship services. Having a landlord relationship with a tenant preserves existing structures and identity. It doesn't challenge one's sense of identity or open the door to the possibility that the future congregation may be predominately Hispanic. Many white urban and suburban churches, even though they bear the community's name, no longer identify with their neighbors. They structure their outreach programs to do missions at a distance rather than develop a relationship with their current neighborhood. They fail to train ushers or members to be open and receptive to visitors whose ethnic or economic background is different. Woven into this unhealthy sense of identity is an unspoken theology that states that the church belongs to its current membership rather than to all those people for whom Christ died.

This leads me to make a rather painful observation: Sometimes the sense of identity that a congregation claims is wrong for its time. Later we shall look at one of the great structural stories of the Old Testament: the tower of Babel. Even now it is important to note that the people began this ill-conceived building project because they wanted to make a name for themselves (Genesis 11:4). The story supports my point that identity is important and that structure can speak volumes about identity. The builders at Babel verbalize the unconscious desires of many church leaders when they say that this tower will keep them from being scattered. Structures provide a gathering place or a format for individuals to express mutually held values and to recognize that they are a community.

Agility

The business world often cites the agility of leadership as the major reason why one business may prosper through an adverse economic climate while other enterprises fail. Agility enables one company to discover new markets, another to recover from a flawed product line, and a third to reduce staff, relocate, or outsource production at the right time. Agility is an important concept for the mainline Protestant church today.

One of the great stories of business agility is Intel's recovery from a faulty math circuit in the Pentium chip in 1994. This is the case of a large, traditional corporation having a very minor flaw in one of its products. They could easily have downplayed the infrequent errors (only one calculation in 27,000 years of regular use would be effected), or promise improvements in the next model. Instead they issued a massive recall. They capitalized on their willingness to exceed their customer's expectations. Significant structural change in the church requires the leaders to both admit the failure of what currently exists and propose solutions that exceed the current congregational expectations.

Most of us have the capacity to be critical of what currently exists around us. Few people have the courage to cultivate the leadership trait that enables us to speak constructively about what needs to be changed. When faced with a problem, we tend to respond defensively. A pastor is confronted about the lack of parking for visitors and responds, "I know that is a problem, and I tried to get the trustees to buy the lot next door, but the money wasn't in the budget. We are doing the best we can with what we have." As you read this book, be aware of the defensive posture you and others adopt about chronic structural issues. Because structural issues are often clearly obvious to outsiders, insiders tend to say, "The brightest and the best of us have thought long and hard about this and it is just the way things have to be." Avoiding the elephant in the room, they focus on ongoing concerns, such as meeting the budget and the text for the next sermon. Solidifying this attitude is the fact that the constituent body is usually okay with the structural failure. The people who pay the bills in the church already know where to park. If a church's leadership sets the agenda to meet the expectations of their current congregation, they will not exhibit much agility.

Agility is the willingness to set short-term transformative goals and then marshal all of the congregation's energy and resources to meet those goals. When the key leaders of a church identify one item as something that is so important that the congregation's future health and survival depends upon it, they have the means and the courage to enlist every resource and group in the church to resolve that issue. Agile churches (and businesses) successfully complete transformative adventures, not just once or twice in a lifetime, but every one to three years.

This definition of agility for the local church has three components:

- the capacity of a few individuals to step back and recognize as critical a single item amid the clutter of daily church life (critical focus);

- an organizational structure that permits the prophetic call of the key leadership team to be communicated as a "do or die" objective to the entire church (unified vision);

- an adventuresome culture that is willing to reorganize repeatedly around a single objective and accomplish the impossible (progressive mindset).

It takes a major crisis for people to step out of their organizational towers. If the furnace dies in January, you will see the finance committee cashing in CDs, the trustees making congregational appeals, and the church school kids rolling pennies. When the new furnace is oversubscribed, the whole affair lapses into the church annuals as a once in a lifetime achievement. For a few brief moments everyone worked

together. Capture this momentum. Make this cooperative spirit and progressive attitude about structural improvements a continuous item on
your congregation's agenda. Then you will know the secret of agility.

Agility requires church leadership to recognize the issues that affect
congregational health, even when they are not as dramatic as a furnace
failure or the loss of a parsonage to a tornado. Consider the matter of
parking cars: A church that does not provide clearly marked parking
spaces for visitors will fail to receive the new members it needs to survive. A caution: Not every church that adds parking spaces grows, but
churches that ignore parking areas will suffer. Agile congregations notice
the gradual effect that inadequate parking has on their potential for
growth.

For the church, agility means a shift in what we expect from our
decision-making bodies. Most churches have expected their leaders to
provide some kind of yearly audit, to do the work of their particular
area, and to inform the whole congregation about a problem only in case
of emergency. The people of Israel expected something similar of King
Saul, until they encountered Goliath. Today every church needs an established process for discovering their most critical issue. Agility only exists
in those organizations that assume that something urgently needs to be
done. They add to their highest governing body a powerful taskforce that
ferrets out the next big challenge. Their culture expects leadershs to communicate the importance of that change and to ground reasons for that
change in mission and ministry.

Agile congregations sense that they are a part of a greater history.
They are not afraid to call their members to sacrifice for a particular
objective or cause. They say, "This is the God-given task of our generation, just as other saints have made their own particular sacrifice for the
kingdom." Their members discover the joy of a constant adrenaline rush,
captured so well by that anonymous author of Hebrews:

> Therefore, since we are surrounded by such a great
> cloud of witnesses, let us throw off everything that hin-
> ders and the sin that so easily entangles, and let us run
> with perseverance the race marked out for us (Hebrews
> 12:1).

Methods for Identifying Critical Issues

Most agile congregations have discovered their own unique mechanism for identifying the next critical issue. A long-term, visionary senior pastor who knows how to communicate boldly what needs to be done next has blessed some. Others intentionally use a designated planning taskforce. This group of six to twelve people is given several months to seriously study the long-term prospects and significant growth obstacles of this church in its current setting. They will study the demographics of the community, as well as the data gathered from recent zoning hearings and real-estate transactions. They try to gain an outsider's perspective as they survey the existing structures, both physical and organizational, of the church. They will seek outside consultants and visit neighboring churches. Such a taskforce should include several new church members, as well as youth. Only a third of the taskforce should be chosen because of their position (such as the pastor); the rest should offer a fresh perspective and creative insights.

Visionary pastors are rare, and most clergy move too often to establish a culture of agility in a congregation. A short-term task force, if it is properly constituted, can achieve remarkable results. They work hard for three to six months to warn the church of future opportunities and challenges. After presenting their report, they disband and let the established leadership of the church implement recommendations. When that particular structural change is achieved, the church council captures the momentum of success and names another taskforce. The process then repeats itself every one to three years, with the duration of the implementation matching the difficulty of the structural change.

When a taskforce brings their recommendation(s) to the church council, sufficient time should be allotted to permit full understanding and a consensus to form around the new priorities of the congregation. Church leadership and the taskforce need to remember that if an easy solution were available, the problem would have been solved long ago. The taskforce process raises to congregational awareness critical issues that call for prayer and reliance upon the resources of God. Once the council is in agreement about the need to meet this challenge, implementation involves total collaboration. The boundaries between the various standing committees are relaxed and new teams are formed to meet the particular challenge. Ideas from a variety of sources are received, and the congregation as a whole joins in prayer about this issue.

The other successful method for implementing structural change and improving the agility of a congregation's leadership is to make continuous use of a church vitality measurement tool. Examples of these include the Church Vitality Indicator, Natural Church Development, and materials from the Alban Institute. These resources help congregations identify strengths and weaknesses to build upon these. Churches that have used these instruments and their related resources also re-evaluate themselves at the end of each year of participation and are thus able to measure change within the congregation's ministry and mission. These evaluative processes help congregations become more agile.

Is Structure the Problem?

I am intrigued by the respectful tone of young David toward the established structures of his society. Saul's military organization is failing to meet the current challenge. David does not criticize their efforts. He proposes an alternative strategy and offers his own skills to implement it (I Samuel 17:32, 34-37). Throughout his life, David's capacity to deal strategically with issues, employing the human resources at hand and not being shackled by role expectations, makes him successful. Even after he has worn the robe of a king for a while, he still has the agility to strip naked and dance to celebrate the return of the Ark of God to Jerusalem (2 Samuel 6:12-14). When David loses this honest naiveté and becomes entangled in the expectations of the royal establishment, he falls prey to the trap of power and sin and leads Israel into tragedy. Both the well-known story of David's involvement with Bathsheba (2 Samuel 11–12) and the lesser-known tale of the great census (2 Samuel 24) are examples of a king complying with expectations of power. Congregational leaders should note that these negative examples stand because David, in almost every other place, wears the mantle of authority so well. His personal spirituality is channeled into a leadership style that intentionally uses prayerful discernment, asking, "What avenue has

God opened up for us in this situation?" Rather than expending energy building status, David communicates to his subordinates the importance of doing the right things at the right time with the right people. Structure is not a problem for David.

Before I became a published writer I always assumed that structure got in the way between the great ideas I had in my head and a best-selling novel. I wanted to write, but I didn't know how to structure my personal life to make time for it. I wanted to write creatively, but the constraints of spelling and grammar seemed to get in the way. I wanted to be published, but the local church structure was a long way from publishing offices.

Since I have begun to write seriously, I entered a more positive relationship with literary structures. I now see that attempting to do something significant with words without structure is like trying to make an omelet without a frying pan. I need to structure my time so that the productive morning hours are set aside for writing. I need to enforce strict rules of punctuation to prevent ambiguity in my communication. Further, I need to be obedient to spiritual structures, such as daily devotions and weekly Sabbath time, to write with discernment and clarity.

The same is true for those who are serious about leadership in the church. The structures that we desire to be free of are the ones we have to embrace and understand in order to change. Like David, we need to cultivate a sensitive heart and a shepherd's intuition to develop alternative structures with integrity. Before a congregation reorganizes its governing board or relocates its ministry, key leaders need to read the pertinent passages of their denominational rulebook. Often one discovers how the lack of compliance to church law in the past has set the stage for the current structural problems.

The local newspaper carried a story about how an effective feeding program offered by a church was shut down by the zoning board when a neighbor sent a complaint letter. It occurs to me that the neighbor would have been unlikely to complain to the zoning board if the church had sought a variance before beginning the ministry. Being aware of the political process would have put the church in a favorable position to act to change their neighborhood. On further reflection, I wonder about the pastor's relationship with the local ministers' group and denominational support structure. When I share what is going on in my church at a regional body, I receive much input in the form of guidance and cautionary warnings about potential pitfalls. When a church's leadership participates in some type of cooperative ministry, they receive the benefit of a learning relationship with other leaders who may have faced similar issues.

Root Causes

Church structures can fail in a variety of ways, but every structural failure involves the following core issues:

- Structures need to be built and maintained with careful consideration as to how they are to grow, adapt to new circumstances, and be replaced. When one is raising money for a project, it is often difficult to keep in mind the transitory nature of all structures. Today's "cutting edge" building will one day be obsolete and will be replaced. We need to remind ourselves constantly that every building is a work in progress. To view even that which is "set in stone" as an organic entity—built to be rebuilt—is the gift of a great leader.

  This becomes even truer with organizational structures. The walls of our committees are not brick and mortar. We can easily modify their composition and duties to meet current reality. Yet many churches find that it would be easier to move the sanctuary a yard to the west than to reduce their church council from twenty-five members to fifteen. The rule of life, for all types of structures, is that what is not made to be flexible is made to die.

- Every structure must be aligned with and supportive of the mission of God and the immediate priorities of the congregation. Congregations often don't know the priorities for their ministry and mission. This is why the administrative committees of a church need to devote time and prayer to discover the congregation's identity and missional vocation. If the leaders do not know what their buildings and committees are meant to support, they are unlikely to create functional structures that will enable their congregation to grow.

When the warning light comes on in my car, I am often stumped as to what is wrong. The "check engine" light may mean a bad fuel filter or a failing transmission. I will take it to the service station and they know what to do. Looking beyond the immediate problem, however, I would be wise to remember the two considerations about structure. Have I maintained the vehicle with a mind towards meeting changing conditions on the roadway? Does the car still get me where I need to go? In looking at structural issues related to a car, we need to step back and see that the whole car may no longer be working. We may need to change the way we make decisions in order to make better decisions. We may need to change our church building in order to save our congregation.

CHAPTER TWO

Engage: When Walls Say Welcome

Test for Stone One: Have You Left the Light On?

Motel 6 has very effective advertisement. Spokesperson Tom Bodett tells people that from the moment they pull in to sleep they will be treated like family. Do the welcoming structures of your church tell people that they are already accepted from the moment that they first turn towards your doors?

This test requires both imagination and a willingness to do outside research. If you are a leader presenting this to a committee, you may want to contact several of your non-church acquaintances and bribe them (yes, it may take a bribe) to spy on your congregation in advance. All they need to do is show up at worship and record their experiences. A British website, Ship of Fools, uses Mystery Worshipers to evaluate churches. You may also invite friends from another church to exchange places with you to evaluate each other's congregation.

Role: You are Jan, a single parent of a ten-year-old boy, who has recently moved into town. You work evenings as a waitress at the local eatery. Saturday night you served an elderly gentleman who tipped you well and invited you to go to his church. The next morning you awoke to see your son in front of the computer playing video games. You say, "Joshua, you and I are going to church!" How easy is it for Jan to find herself in worship?

1) If Jan types the name of your church and your town into Google, will she quickly find a web page that gives her a map and a current listing of your worship times? (Check this out before answering.)

No church web page = -1
Web page exists but is hard to find or inaccurate = 0
An inviting web page in first 20 hits of Google = 1

2) As Jan pulls off the roadway with a vague notion of where your church is, how easy is it for her to find the church entrance and to know where to park? (Ask a person who has never attended your church to try this out at five minutes before your primary worship time.)

A little confusing = 0   Real easy = 1

3) A few minutes before worship begins, are there any empty parking spaces, clearly marked for visitors, within 100 feet of your church entrance? (Some type of valet parking and/or managed drop-off zone wins you extra credit on this one.)

No = -2
Yes = 1
Greeters standing outside to help with parking = 2
(extra credit)

4) From the parking lot to the pew, are there people trained and prepared to help Jan feel welcomed and to answer any questions she may have? (Training must be done at least every six months.)

No = 0   Yes = 1

5) If Jan and Joshua arrived five minutes after the worship began, how positive and helpful would their reception be? (Again, have a non-church member try this out.)

No one at the door = 0
Greeter with welcoming smile = 1

6) If they entered the church by the wrong door, is there enough signage to help them find their way to the sanctuary? What about signage for restrooms, fellowship space, and children's ministry areas around the building?

> No = 0   Yes = 1

7) What things would positively engage Joshua, the ten-year-old, on his first Sunday morning with you? What is visually appealing to a child in the entrance or worship space? What is said or done for children during worship?

> Nothing "kid friendly" about the experience = -1
> A children's "keep them busy" activity pack = 0
> Parts of the worship and visual items specifically
> designed to engage children = 1

8) Imagine that Joshua is in a wheelchair. What will Jan and Joshua experience as they arrive to worship at your church? (Include the accessibility of restrooms in your evaluation.)

> Any Barrier (Steps, Inaccessible Restrooms, etc) = -5
> Assessable, but not clearly marked = 0
> Signs and knowledgeable greeters providing access
> without embarrassment = 1
> (Additional extra credit if you offer services for the
> deaf)

9) Are the announcements presented in such a way that Jan and Joshua feel invited to attend the church's public activities? (Again, have an outsider listen to your announcements and critically mark-up your bulletin. They should be honest about the tone and clarity of the announcements. They should note announcements which fail to clearly state the time, location, cost, and purpose of the event.)

> No = 0
> Yes = 1
> Use of LCD visuals or skits to present key announcements = 2 (extra credit)

10) Of the people on your church council, including pastor(s) and staff, how many of them would be likely to tip well and offer the waitress an invitation to church?

No = 0   Yes = 1

11) Do you offer training to church members on how to speak about their faith?

No = 0   Yes = 1

12) Is the landscape around the church well kept and varied from year to year?

No = 0   Yes = 1

13) Do you make use of the seasons, particularly Christmas and Easter, to invite people into a relationship with your church?

No = 0   Yes = 1

14) Is something new done to the outward appearance of your church every year?

No = 0   Yes = 1

15) What new thing have you started to do this year to engage the non-church attending culture?

Nothing = 0
One minor change or activity = 1
Major effort or outreach = 2

Score for Stone One: _____

This test has a possible score of fifteen (plus 3 extra credits) which can be multiplied times 6.6 to give you a recognizable grade; 90-100 "A", 80-89 "Good, but room for improvement," 70-79 "passing", 60 and below "You are failing to leave the light on." Compare this score with the other tests to give your leadership a sense as to which structures are functional and which ones don't fit your church's mission. You will see Jan and Joshua again.

When Walls Say, Welcome

"So I say to you: Ask and it will be given to you; seek and you will find; knock and the door will be opened to you."

Luke 11:9

"If you are searching for something to believe in; our hearts, our minds, and our doors are always open."

Igniting Ministries Media campaign (United Methodist Communications, 2004)

Engage

Whenever Captain Kirk takes the starship *Enterprise* out to explore the cosmos, he issues a single command: "Engage." What follows is always an adventure. In some episodes, frightening alien creatures take over the ship, shutting down propulsion and life-support. The captain and crew struggle not only to get essential systems back online, but also to understand what these strangers want and how to reason with them. The captain seeks to open a channel of communication so he can tell them that mission of the ship is peaceful. If he can engage this alien culture, then perhaps he can build a level of trust that will spare the *Enterprise* from further attacks and perhaps initiate a mutually beneficial exchange of knowledge. What makes Captain Kirk such a good leader is that he wants to understand the universe. His posture is receptive, not defensive, and his inner vision leads him to look beyond the current crisis. The ship's entire crew is organized with exploration in mind. Further, the physical vessel is outfitted with a wide variety of sensors and probes. "Engage" is not just a command; it is a state of mind.

Jesus called the church to engage the world. Jesus said we are to be in the world, even if we are not to be of it (John 17:15-18). He told Peter that the keys to the kingdom are such that the gates of Hell itself will not stand against the church (Matthew 16:18-19). The attacks that the church experiences will sometime lead us to think we need to seek refuge and emphasize the disparity between Christian values and those held by those who are not Christian. The Bible, however, frames the church's mission in terms of engagement. Jesus said, " . . . you will receive power when the Holy Spirit comes on you; and you will be my witnesses in Jerusalem, and in all Judea and Samaria, and to the ends of the earth." Early church leadership captained a costly program of active engagement with a sometimes-hostile culture. Their mission was not simply to survive, but to explore and to witness.

Many congregations have retreated from the postmodern culture. Their weekly communal life is cloistered behind an unwelcoming façade. Rather than helping them to engage the world, the church walls, signage, advertisements, and parking facilities conspire to communicate the congregation's desire to be separate. Reflect for a few moments about the visual appearance of your church buildings. Many urban "First Church" type congregations have inherited a fortress-like architecture that makes their building look like a medieval castle. The uninitiated would be surprised to find a welcome behind these buttressed walls, stone towers, deep-set tinted windows, and ambiguous marquees. These churches may even have slotted roof parapets that make me think at any moment a band of archer will appear to repel all intruders. This non-verbal message is the only message most passersby have from the church. The identity and cultural expectations of your congregation has been shaped by its defensive architecture.

What do the main doors of your sanctuary say about your fellowship? Do they express a sense of transparency? When young adults speak about what they are looking for in a religious gathering, they speak about honesty, authenticity, and the willingness of a group to share itself with the world. Many churches, however, have retained their old fortress doors. These oversized, heavy, oaken monstrosities non-verbally communicate the congregation's fixation upon safety and security. Those who safely make it through these doors are promised refuge from the dangers outside. Those who belong to today's culture, however, do not seek withdrawal. They value the free exchange of ideas within today's media rich society. They seek relevance rather than sanctuary, which unfortunately is the most salient feature of Victorian church architecture (1830 to 1920). Four generations later, the church needs to engage a very different culture. Instead of looking for a place to get away, contemporary people want a church that will provide them with tools for living within the world.

This same change in architectural style is visible in bank buildings built before 1960 and those opened more recently. The early twentieth century bank architecture communicated stability and impregnability. Stone façades and fortress-like elements helped make people feel their investments were safe. The massive locking mechanisms of bank vaults were visible from bank lobbies. These visual details were designed so customers got the message, "The money you deposit here will never be stolen." Today's culture looks for a very different kind of financial institution. The old architecture is rapidly being replaced. Stone edifices are being torn down and replaced by glass and tubular aluminum. Lobbies no longer display vaults, but information counters and computer terminals. LCD screens are in. Drive-up services and brightly lit all-hour ATM machines receive top billing. People today don't choose a new bank because it offers them a sense of security; we choose banks that are convenient and provide the services we need.

In 1968 Emory Church burned down as a result of arson. The congregation now had the opportunity to replace their fortress-like structure with something modern. They thought about security because of the arson. They built a beautiful and highly functional building. The new façade no longer looks like a medieval castle; now it has no windows that face the street. The architect, instead, gave the congregation their own private courtyard. While the building is modern, secure, and comfortable to those inside, nothing about its exterior says, "Welcome." Since moving into the new building the congregation has been in decline, struggling to attract newcomers. Church structures can be modern, functional, and well designed, but unless they help the congregation engage the culture, they are outdated.

Having an unwelcoming façade is not simply a minor disadvantage to a church; it is a major cultural roadblock. I believe the primary function of our walls and doors is to advertise our presence in the world.

We must use the exterior of our buildings to engage the culture. The landscape should be continuously updated and include eye-catching, colorful flowers. Seasonal banners can take the edge off of ancient walls. My town's sports team colors are not liturgical colors, but when the Steelers made the Super Bowl some churches chose to communicate, "We are fun, not formal," with black and gold exterior displays. Given a blank wall today and an active church, I might suggest an LED display with scrolling messages. Our church walls need to show hospitality as we engage the culture in Christian mission. We need to find ways to communicate, verbally and non-verbally, that we receive people just as they are.

Giving Up the Fort

Does this mean that we have to forsake our familiar cathedral walls? What if we are a main street church in a town whose people shop at the suburban mall? Many congregations abandoned aging downtown buildings and moved to the suburbs. Some new church starts are renting non-church structures (storefronts, schools, movie theaters) to attract people. The question really comes down to context and timing. Doing an honest assessment may lead you to conclude that the time for flight is past. Your congregation may no longer have the resources to relocate nor may you discern that the Holy Spirit would permit you to abandon your particular corner.

On the other hand, your congregation may have already relocated or built new in the past forty years and you are wondering what to do now. Structures need continuous modification to remain current. While recently built buildings don't look like ancient forts, they can present that subliminal message if they lack good signage, adequate parking, fresh landscaping, and inviting doorways. Cultural doorways, such as web presence, involvement in the community, and opportunities for non-attenders to use the facilities, are as important as physical entrances. Having a relatively new building does not free a congregation from being vigilant about the welcoming nature of their structures.

There are very few congregations with buildings so historically important or that make such a unique architectural contribution that they deserve to be preserved in their current state. Congregations living in these structures may make many sacrifices to preserve the old. For every legitimate historic icon there are a hundred church buildings that have outlived their usefulness. If your building does not rate a spot on the Landmark Society's register, then you must take a pragmatic view of it. The current religious climate is not one in which the church can be sentimental about the old days. What no longer serves the mission of the church must be disposed of because it impedes our witness. Stained glass can be sold and pipe organs removed. Only God is holy—nothing else. Failure to remember this holiness as we contemplate our religious structures is a subtle form of idolatry that leads to many missed opportunities. Failing to remain current leads to decline and decline eventually results in the loss of the congregation. The business consultant W. Edwards Deming, who was instrumental in the reconstruction of Japan after World War Two, put it this way, "It is not necessary to change. Survival is not mandatory."

For most mid-sized and smaller churches (less than 200 in worship attendance) an intentional, long-range planning process would discern the importance of remaining in the same neighborhood and the importance of being willing to make significant changes to the facility. Some churches would do well to rent a different space for weekly worship and convert their current corner facility into a seven-day-a-week space for mission outreach. Others should divide their sanctuary, creating a functional, intimate, modern worship setting, which is the appropriate size for its current congregation, and then renting out the portion that remains. Still others need to totally remodel their exteriors to present a more welcoming face to those outside.

Where to Begin

Jesus talks about how the kingdom of God belongs to those who, like little children, see things differently (Matthew 18:3-4). One interpretation of this is that doing religion involves breaking free from preconceptions. Whether we are seeking salvation for our souls or a way to make our walls more welcoming, we must intentionally rig our process to create what the Zen masters call "beginner's mind." How would we see our church building if we had never seen a church before? What are the things that the congregation does that would be mystifying to the new attendee? Is there anything jarring or off-putting in our greeting routine? Do church representatives at the door, both coming and going, come off as sincere and authentic? Is it easy to be lost or locked out if you don't have someone guiding you?

The place to begin is with a short-term task force whose only task is to identify six to ten ways your current walls are unwelcoming. As in the previous section on implementing agility (see chapter one: *"Methods for Identifying Critical Issues"*) this group should include six to twelve people chosen for their potential to think creatively rather than for their current role as church leaders. Half of the people should be relatively new to the congregation. They should start by working through the questionnaire at the beginning of this chapter. They should discuss the low scoring questions, not to provide solutions, but to create a list of priorities. This task force, which should complete its work in three or four meetings, will create a list and provide verbal support for their conclusions. The list may be presented in random order or with the most unwelcoming aspect of the church at the top. They should be instructed not to order their list in terms of feasibility and not to worry about any political ramifications of these changes.

The task force should visit neighboring churches. The purpose of these visits is to experience barriers even the best churches present to the stranger. Most of us only attend a church other than our own when we are visiting relatives. To know what visitors feel, one needs to go alone into an unfamiliar sanctuary a few minutes after the service is scheduled to begin.

The task force and the church council as a whole will have a much easier time identifying a list of specific projects if they invite several outsiders to visit your church for one Sunday and then talk about their experience. The challenge is to receive these candid reports without becoming defensive. Develop a list of explorative questions based on the questionnaire at the beginning of this chapter. How do the answers the visitors provide differ from the results you have from your church's leaders? Train your ear to hear what is said after, "your church is very nice, *but* . . . " This simple task of asking three or four people to visit and give you a critical report is likely to be more beneficial to your leadership than attending a "church growth" seminar. Because it yields specific results, however, it is both easy to apply and easy to dismiss. Getting into the mind of unchurched Jan and Joshua is difficult, but the exercise pays ample dividends. I am convinced that it is this cultural bias towards the non-member, rather than church size or theology, which marks the vibrant and growing congregations of our era.

Focus all of the church's energy on solving one critical issue at a time and then move from success to success, conquering all the ways your walls don't welcome strangers. The goal is to develop a progressive mindset that continuously improves the congregation's skills at engaging the culture. A single improvement, such as improving parking, may not bring a noticeable increase in worship attendance. However, we cannot claim to have a welcoming, friendly congregation if strangers don't know where to park. Congregational culture will not change without congregational action.

Isaac Newton observed that a body in motion tends to remain in motion and a body at rest remains at rest until acted on by an outside force. The outside forces that influence resting congregations today are rarely positive. Those leaders who value agility and keep their people directed towards doing the things that can be done are less likely to be caught flat-footed by change.

Working on Your Walls

The projects that improve the welcoming nature of a congregation fall into four general areas:

CURB APPEAL

Does your church exterior look like the home of a lively congregation? Would the average drive-by church shopper think it worth investigating? Planting flowers or painting the trim a contrasting color may make a significant difference in appeal. Churches tend to err on the side of conservative color schemes and exteriors. Whatever exterior lighting you think is appropriate, double it. Pick trim colors with an eye towards making a bold statement, rather than choosing what we all can live with. The goal is not to maintain congregational harmony, but to be noticed by the person passing by. "Engage the culture" is the motto for all landscaping decisions.

COMMUNICATION

How do unchurched Jan and Joshua know when to come to your worship services? What if Jan was interested in the single-parent support group offered by your church? I used to note with disgust how many churches had marquees that were misleading, unattractive, or failed to tell the time of this week's services. Now, I am convinced that just having an up-to-date church sign is not enough. People go to many different sources for information. Welcoming congregations intentionally target three to five information channels to promote worship service times and style (for example casual dress or worship in Korean and English), times and contact numbers for 12-Step programs and other activities, confidential crisis-lines or intercessory prayer groups, and seasonal events.

Here are some information channels:

1. A well-lit church marquee with current worship times, web address, and contact phone number.

2. The off-hours phone answering service (make sure the voice-mail system is easy to navigate.). A dedicated church phone line should greet every caller with a way to get current worship and event times, as well as other extensions to reach key locations, such as the kitchen, fellowship hall, office, and a prayer or crisis line.

3. The church website. A well-designed web page is cheaper than traditional print media and more informative. Plan to update the information on your website every week.

4. Creative alternatives: If you hope to reach out to immigrants and have bilingual or multilingual worship services, buy advertising space on the placemats and menus of ethnic restaurants in the area. If you are reaching out to students at a college, advertise on campus and in coffee shops they frequent.

5. Billboards, radio spots, and public transportation placards.

6. Another information channel is on the slides shown in theaters before movies. The weeks prior to the beginning of school, Christmas, and Easter are fertile times for inviting people to a special event or "seeker oriented" worship experience.

Church leaders need to think in terms of multiple communication channels to provide essential information to support outreach. Seeing information in several outlets may help convince someone to visit your church.

Churches also need to make more creative use of flyers and event handouts. What if the layperson who invited the waitress Jan had a small business card that listed the church service times and contact information? When you plan this year's Lenten study or special Easter services, will you place all of the relevant information (including a map) in a flyer or bookmark? How good is your distribution channel for posters and handbills? Can you inspire church members to offer a flyer to the person on the next treadmill at the Y? Do you distribute information in the lobby of the local senior high rise? Devote a lot of attention to developing an attractive print format, with a distinctive and consistent logo, that works for your congregation and location. Get a variety of people involved in designing the first edition of your special event flyer. Build ownership across the congregation for the chosen forms of advertising by involving many people in their creation. Using the same basic format over and over not only saves time; it encourages committee chairs to be more conscientious about advertising their programs. Shift the church's culture so that every leader believes that if a program is worth doing, it's worth advertising.

PARKING AND ACCESSIBILITY

Why would a new person expect to walk farther to come to your church doors than they do to their grocery store? How confusing is it for them to find a parking space? If they have a disability or handicapping condition, what barriers will they encounter in your building and in your church culture? What about the restrooms? If your church offers signing for the deaf or bilingual worship, are these services advertised?

Often church leaders will view the above questions in terms of a series of obligations. We are required to meet certain codes under the Americans with Disabilities Act (1990) for new construction. We ought to provide a certain number of parking spaces for our membership. This mode of thinking segregates parking and accessibility as side issues to the real activities of the church. The presumption of this mindset is that loyalty to a particular denomination or tradition will keep people supporting this church, even it is physically inconvenient for them or puts them at risk of embarrassment.

This is a dangerous and theologically questionable attitude. We live in a culture that views unimpeded access into and ease of travel within public buildings as a matter of common courtesy. If an organization fails to provide a ramp to its main meeting space or forces its patrons to climb stairs to use the restroom, it is considered an act of callous rudeness. My sense is that younger adults, because they are extremely relationship oriented as a generation, are mindful of the barriers a structure would impose upon their disabled friends and family members even when those people are not there. Meanwhile, older adults and the disabled are loosing their patience with churches that offer halfway solutions. If the only way one can attend church is to dangle precariously on a chairlift up a circular staircase, leaving wheelchair or walker below for someone else to carry up, that person will choose to stay home. Society as a whole has raised the bar on convenience for both restrooms and parking.

In thinking about accessibility one should consider the needs of three other groups; those caring for small children or infants, those with visual impairments, and those with hearing loss. Meeting the needs of these people is not a matter of investing large sums of money, but of gaining an appreciation of their church experience. Your church may already offer some type of personal amplification device, but are the receiving units displayed in a convenient location, have their batteries been checked, and are there enough of them? Is the fact that a service for hearing impaired individuals exists communicated in three forms—in the bulletin each week, on a sign near the sanctuary door, and by the trained ushers? In a similar fashion, do you provide large print bulletins and hymnals and have you trained your ushers to offer them? It only takes a slight visual impairment to make a stair tread invisible, especially during an evening service. Take the time to note what might be dangerous to a person who is unfamiliar with the church's terrain and install contrasting carpet, warning signs, and floor lighting where needed. In a similar fashion, those caring for infants expect to find a child-safe environment, with changing stations clearly marked. Many also need the freedom to come and go from the service to meet the needs of the child. The ushering staff once again becomes the primary communicator of the congregation's support for these people.

It is interesting to note the lengths secular businesses will go to provide convenient parking for their patrons. If a popular nightclub lacks safe parking, they will hire a valet service to shuttle the cars to a distant location. Airports and amusement parks provide shuttle buses. Rarely will a landlocked business pass up the opportunity to purchase adjacent land and increase parking. Unlike church leaders, those in business know the value that each parking space brings to the business. To determine the value of a church parking space take the annual budgeted income of your church from general offerings and divide by the number of parking spaces you currently own or have uncontested access to. For example, if you receive $150,000 in offering income each year and have 50 parking spaces, then the value of each space is $3,000 per year. This formula works because one can safely assume that only those people who regularly find parking spaces are able to give. If a new family drives by your church because they were unable to find parking, the cost of losing them amounts to $3,000 per year. Similarly, if a shuttle service costing

$15,000 per year allows ten people to leave their car at the high-rise, it has paid for itself twice over. If an adjacent property costs $90,000 and offers room for ten cars, it will pay for itself in three years if the parking was needed. Church leaders often assume that parking is an unsolvable problem. They need to do the math and meet the challenge head on.

SIGNAGE

Poor signage comes in three forms: missing, confusing, and insulting. It amazes me how often churches fail to point the way to their parking lot or provide a clear indication of what form of worship will be offered at what times. If your church offers a service to people with a special need, such as a barrier free entry, non-English language support, valet parking, the time and/or location of these offerings should be clearly signed. Parking for visitors as well as the mid-week entry door should also be marked. Restrooms often need several signs, not only to insure that their location and gender is visible when the hallway is crowded, but also to lead people toward restrooms from the lobby, sanctuary, and meeting rooms.

Confusing signage often takes the form of church jargon. If you want the Boy Scout troop leader, who is not from your congregation, to be able to find a mop when he needs it, then clearly mark the janitor's closet and leave the items related to spill cleanup unlocked. Having all supplies hidden behind a door marked "Sexton," "Storage" or "Room 101" is confusing. Church jargon also includes words such as *narthex*, *rectory*, and *vestibule*. Invite a taskforce to evaluate your church signage every two or three years. Long-time church members may name certain rooms after the class that used to meet there, but someone needs to devise and maintain a naming convention that is flexible and visitor friendly. Larger churches need to consider posting maps or adopting a color scheme to aid visitors. Good signage requires creativity and a willingness to spell out plainly what members consider obvious.

Insulting signs include those hand-lettered notes that well-intentioned church members post to control the actions of others. One church kitchen had no indication as to where I might find a spoon, but there were several signs warning me to stay out the woman's society's cupboard. Another church had so many "no smoking" signs that I wondered if it had become one of the Ten Commandments.

When Is a Door Not a Door?

When Andrew Carnegie endowed millions of dollars to build new library buildings, he had them place over the doorway four words that captured his dream: "Free to the Public." Writing something on the doorway has been a classic way for institutions to summarize how what happens within their walls will affect the lives of those who dare to enter. In Deuteronomy the families of Israel were told to place the commandment to love the Lord their God at the doorways of their homes (Deuteronomy 6:1-9). This act proclaims that the family institution is the place where learning about God will occur.

It may not be appropriate for you to write something above your church entrance, but thinking about what message you hope to convey to those who enter is a worthwhile exercise for your church council. How do you set the tone for worship, fellowship, and religious study? You may want to consider adding an architectural detail near your entrance, such as a banner, fountain, or sculpture. Clear glass doors opening into a well lit, cheery narthex can promote a feeling of accessibility.

Look at the messages displayed near your entrance. The first time attendee is highly influenced by the subliminal. If the parking spaces nearest your front doors have signs saying the spaces are reserved for clergy and staff, then you are proclaiming a hierarchical value set. Visitors are put on notice that they will be considered to be second-class. One struggling church near me has a lovely, bright, colorful sign in its yard for the preschool that rents its building throughout the week. The adjacent church marquee is a dull black formal affair with gothic lettering. The people who may have been enticed onto the property by the preschool know that the views of the church are different than those of their child-friendly preschool.

What are the doors or pathways through which a stranger might pass on their way to becoming a part of your congregation? Word of mouth or personal invitations are likely to be the most engaging way in which people discover your church. It is important to cultivate a congregational culture that is passionate about inviting others to join in worship. Another doorway is paid advertisement and a web presence. A third door may be the invitation extended to outside groups who use or rent your facilities. Even when your congregation has a purely business relationship with the people using a space, one can tactfully let their clients know they are welcome to participate in any of the church's activities.

Postmodern Values

The reason this discussion about inviting doors and welcoming walls is critical for so many churches is because of the great cultural change that occurred in the last half of the twentieth century. The things a congregation must do today to gain and retain active members are very different from what worked in the 1950s. It is hard to overstate this change. As one who received a traditional seminary education in the mid-1970s, I sometimes feel like an athlete who trained and prepared to play football, and then found that the only game is soccer. Even though church is still church, the game and rules we must obey today are entirely different. Some of our most beloved church structures have been created to serve a dwindling demographic. We need to engage the culture we have, not the culture we wish for. We need to adapt our structures for our current reality, not for what used to be.

Briefly stated, there are three cultural shifts that affect our church structures:

- **Membership is no longer valued.** People no longer participate in anything because they want to be thought of as *good members*. People today participate in what they find to be relevant, meaningful, and convenient. Instead of inviting people to "join us" in our institution, we need to help people to experience the value of Christian faith for their lives.

- **People today distrust hierarchy.** While I think my own denomination is right to retain a structure that delineates distinct roles for bishops, district superintendents, clergy, and lay people, this is not the face of Methodism I present to the world. It is like underwear, important to have, but best to be hidden. I rarely use the title *Reverend,* and I avoid any implication that there is an authority pyramid in the church.

- **Everybody is searching for community and authentic relationships.** This should be good news for the church. What we have to share with the world is not a storehouse of religious knowledge, but a joyous fellowship that revolves around the grace of God and the love we can have for our neighbors.

Beneath all of the technical complexities of today's world there are human hearts yearning for simplicity. The pre-1960 structures of the church focused upon complex rules for membership, hierarchical institutional values, and a rational ordering system that segmented people into distinct classes. If only we can once again express the simplicity of Jesus' gospel through intentionally revamped structures, then we will have no problem expanding the church in the postmodern age.

Many congregations will need to abandon their current facilities in order to become more welcoming to this culture. The greater shift, however, will need to be in the way congregations think about their structures. We will need to see our church buildings and committees as temporary vessels, useful for transporting the gospel, but failing to express the loving heart of our faith. It is my conclusion that the reason so many churches fail to keep pace in modifying their outward appearance is not because they lack the finances, but because they have become alienated from modern culture. They distrust it and assume that younger adults have lost the desire to be religious. I think we need to engage the people who inhabit the streets of our cities, rather than pay homage to those who have gone on to their reward in heaven. We need to embrace the modern values of simplicity, transparency, authenticity, and diversity with the same zeal that we once embraced the modern age values of rationality, order, certainty, and homogeneity.

CHAPTER THREE

Nurture: Where People Learn to Love the Lord

Test for Stone Two: Will They Come Back?

Imagine that it is the Sunday after Christmas. Jan, a single mother of a ten-year-old boy, wants to enroll him in your Sunday school. Joshua is not as enthusiastic about this New Year's resolution as his mother. In fact, he uses his most recently acquired new word, "hypocritical," to describe his mother's sudden interest in religion. He can only remember being taken to church twice before. Talking to his grandmother he has discovered that mom wasn't forced to go to church as a kid. Why should he be made to do this? He arrives on your church's doorstep expecting two hours of boredom. Jan, meanwhile, is not sure what she will be doing while she waits for worship. Can you interest her in some type of adult learning experience? More importantly, will both the educational and worship experience meet both of their spiritual needs?

I) If Jan drops Joshua off at the church, are there people who will insure he arrives at the age appropriate class?

___ (-1) No church school offered.

___ (0) Classes happen, but not much thought has been given to those who arrive after the official start of the Sunday school year.

___ (1) A welcoming person notices newcomers and is prepared to provide information and assurances to parents who are dropping kids off.

2) How many of the following information sources are actually working in your church: (1 point for each.)

___ Exterior sign(s) tells the time of Sunday school and worship services.

___ Web page lists current class offerings with time and description for both children and adults.

___ Phone call to the main church number during business hours will connect a caller to a person who can accurately describe all of the worship and study options offered by the church.

___ Phone call during off hours connects caller with voice mail or a message service that provides frequently updates listings of study and worship times.

3) As Jan attends worship at your church, how is she encouraged to participate in an adult learning experience? (1 point for each.)

___ The people who lead worship frequently express the congregation's commitment to life-long learning.

___ The bulletin accurately lists this week's study opportunities (who is invited, what is studied, where the class is located and how long the class is).

___ Jan will receive numerous personal invitations to participate in a study experience.

___ When Jan inquires about joining the church, she will be informed that participation in a weekly study experience is an expectation for all church members.

4) What is the current percentage of participation of your worshipers in study groups? To find this, divide your average weekly worship attendance by the number of distinct individuals who attend a study experience (don't count the same person more than once), and then divide 100 by this number to convert into a percentage. For example:

120 people in worship / 60 individuals attending classes = 2

100 / 2 = 50% religious education participation

Less than 20 % = -1 point

20 to 40 % = 0 points

41 to 60 % = 1 point

61 to 100 % = 2 points

5) Have you formed a new small group in the last six months?

Yes = 1 point

No = 0 points

Additional point if you offer a new study experience every six to nine weeks

6) How well is worship integrated into the church school experience?

   __ Those who provide childcare and/or a children's class during worship miss the opportunity to worship half the weeks of the year. (-1 point)

   __ The church school and the worship team operate as two separate entities. (0 points)

   __ Church school is designed to teach children how to worship (1 point)

   __ There is a constant cross fertilization between worship and the educational experience of children and adults. The church leadership intentionally links growth in faith and knowledge with the participation in worship. (2 points)

7) Is regular participation in a small group for learning and prayer a stated prerequisite for church leadership? Do all of your church council members attend some form of religious education (adult church school class, Bible study, covenant prayer group, etc.)?

    No = 0   Yes = 1

8) Do you make use of the seasons, particularly the first day of school, New Years, and Lent to invite people into recommit to religious education?

    No = 0   Yes = 1

9) Is your worship experience ordered so as to capture the emotional quality of our spiritual lives? Is it inspiring on a "gut-level"?

    No = 0   Yes = 1

10) Is the Bible presented with relevance during worship? Do the scripture readers take a moment to set the lesson in its context and prepare the congregation to understand what they will be hearing?

No = 0   Yes = 1

11) Inspect the spaces used by your church for small group learning experiences. For each classroom score from -1 to +1 in terms of safety, cleanliness, comfort, and attractiveness. Be specifically mindful of the group(s) that will be using that room. Then do an overall assessment:

Poor = -2   -1   0   + 1   Excellent = +2
(Many rooms need repairs)   (Ok)   (Functional and attractive)

12) If Jan were to visit your church's worship, what specific things would she experience that might intrigue her to return the next week? (Score 1 point for each item that you can name up to 3 points.)

13) If Jan were to attend one of your adult classes or bible studies, what specific things would she experience that might intrigue her to return the next week? (Score 1 point for each item that you can name up to 3 points, score -1 if you do not offer a regular weekly educational experience for adults.)

Score for Stone two: _____

The raw score for Stone Two can be multiplied times five to give you a recognizable grade; 90-100 "Excellent", 80-89 "Good, but room for improvement," 70-79 "passing", etc. If you score below 60, chances are that you are not doing what you need to do to help others come to know and love the Lord.

Jesus invited his disciples into an intense small group experience so they might associate the things they were learning about God with the experience of participating in a loving fellowship. The message (God's grace) and the medium (a loving fellowship) are always linked in the life of a congregation. As a church fails to do nurture well, its internal relationships cool and it fails to perform Jesus' command that we love one another. This downward spiral denies the church the energy and resources it needs to provide comfortable educational facilities and to recruit good teachers and worship leaders.

Structuring a Place for People to Learn to Love the Lord

. . . the earth will be full of the knowledge of the LORD
as the waters cover the sea.

Isaiah 11:9

After three days they found him [the twelve year old, Jesus] in the temple courts, sitting among the teachers, listening to them and asking them questions. Everyone who heard him was amazed at his understanding and his answers . . . "Why were you searching for me?" he asked. "Didn't you know I had to be in my Father's house?"

Luke 2:46-47, 49

Plot

Nurture is the church's plot. Many people who attempt to write fiction find their greatest difficulty in developing the plot of a story. Plot makes a reader want to turn to the next page and read more. People describe a good book as one that they can't put down. John Grisham and J. K. Rowling are examples of authors who know how to structure the events of their books to build audience participation. In the church, nurture keeps people returning to the church, not only for one hour a week, but also for major portions of their free time. Nurture engages the young and the irreligious and makes them interested in the things of God. Like the writer's craft, it must be carefully structured to capture the imagination and convey the things that are most critical for living faith-filled lives.

Nurturing churches keep people coming back by providing returns for the time spent. When we find our worship or small group time has enabled us to glimpse the divine or transcend the ordinary, we want to return. We go to church and hope to see the reign of God advance and God's will be done on earth as it is done in heaven. Vital churches constantly improve the structures they use to lift the human spirit, build communion with the divine, and inform people about the nature of their spiritual warfare.

The chance that people will understand the church's plot is significantly improved when the facilities are comfortable and appropriate to the nurturing experience. A drafty basement classroom can make the most riveting Bible study fall flat. In every city in America, cavernous sanctuaries with their poor acoustics drown out many otherwise wonderful worship experiences. One should never assume that a wonderful presenter can overcome inadequate audio-visual equipment or a failing facility.

People also continue reading books for the sake of the characters in the book. Character development is to the writer's craft what fellowship or Christian community is to the church. Unless we emotionally connect (even if it is on a negative level) with the people we read about, we are reluctant to wade through the details of their experiences and stay tuned to the end of their conflicts. Fellowship supports nurture. To use another metaphor, fellowship provides the glue that keeps us stuck together through the ups and downs of spiritual life. It is one of the things that the small membership congregation has it its favor as it seeks to win new members in today's adverse religious climate. The communal structure of a healthy church meets a deep yearning in the hearts of people of every age and status.

Good Conflict

Many church leaders strive hard to avoid conflict, but conflict is essential to every plot and is a defining aspect of healthy spiritual nurture. Conflict exists in each of our lives because we are earthbound creatures with heaven-oriented values. The church must position itself in the middle of this paradox. People come to church and have had a number of confusing or troubling experiences. One person may have learned about a life-threatening disease while several may experience difficult marriages and still others face ethical dilemmas in the work place. A church's nurturing environment provides a safe place to move the issues out from the subconscious and into awareness. More importantly, church juxtaposes the particular experience of the individual against the backdrop of scripture and the communion of the saints, past and present. Terminally ill people see their sufferings in the context of eternal glory, while those in conflicted marriages may see the relationship in the context of our ongoing need for forgiveness and reconciliation. You and I know countless examples. Through all of this, the church carries on Jesus' work.

When King Solomon dedicated the temple, he envisioned it as a place where people could bring the discordant aspects of their lives and find healing through prayer (2 Chronicles 6:21-41). Many congregations today have abandoned their nurturing role by creating a wall between the drama of daily life and the ritual of religious practice. This insulation against conflict is sometimes supported by a perfectionist attitude. By way of contrast, one of my favorite churches prominently displays boxes of tissues on its altar rail and encourages its leaders to come and weep with those who seek intercession.

Church leaders need to structure each nurturing experience so as to maintain a healthy recognition of the conflicts we each encounter in life. Adult classes and small groups need to be designed so that time is provided for people to express their prayer needs. When instructional content consistently squeezes out intercessory prayer, the false notion is promulgated that faith is a purely rational thing. Ideally, a church strives to provide a variety of small groups, and encourages different comfort levels of sharing. On the other hand, people have a right to privacy and care needs to be exercised to insure that no one feels forced beyond their comfort level. In maintaining this balance the following things should be kept in mind.

Each age level has its own security and personal vulnerability issues. Children need to be protected from manipulative and predatory adults. Background checks must be done on all who have contact with youth and children, not only from a risk-management point of view, but with an awareness of the peculiar vulnerability that undergirds the faith sharing experience. Team teaching at every age level enables the Christian education department to intentionally develop a nurturing culture that is authentic, transparent, and consistent.

For both youth and adults, the level of personal vulnerability is directly related to the length of time a group has met together without a major change in membership. This means that people will only legitimately share their deepest fears and experiences with a group they have come to know and trust. Youth leaders are sometimes tempted to manipulate the emotions of their group to get them to "open up." Co-dependent and intrusive teachers are common in today's congregations. Churches do well to establish a procedure for ongoing supervision, training, and peer review of every educational leader.

Small groups should be designated as either "open chair" or "covenant" by their structure. An open chair group is one that is intentionally seeking new participants and will receive new members at any point. In fact, their leadership should be constantly aware of the need to advertise and promote an invitational culture, hence to "fill the open chair." Most church fellowship groups and classes should be designed to grow up to a certain size, and then divide into two groups. Replication is the key sign of a healthy structure for "open chair" type classes. Most church school classes and short-term learning experiences in the church today fall into this category. It is rare, however, to see their leaders being as diligent as they should be about welcoming new attenders.

"Covenant groups" are small groups (fewer than twelve participants) that, after a few meetings, become closed to new members. They may on special occasions add an outsider, but the emphasis of the group is that they grow to trust one another. Because it can achieve a higher level of vulnerability, this structure is appropriate for 12-Step type programs and for groups that meet the needs of at-risk youth. Covenant groups are also appropriate for people who wish to hold each other to greater accountability for their ethical and spiritual lives. The *L3 Incubator* (Discipleship Resources) process has also demonstrated the effectiveness of covenant groups for developing a new leadership culture in the church.

Many churches fail to appreciate this fundamental structural difference that relates to the vulnerability participants bring to their class relationships. Community in any setting is built in three distinct steps.

First, a group gathers around interest in particular subject matter or content. This first step is common to open chair and covenant groups, but open chair groups cannot go very far into the next level of community. Second, the group agrees (preferably through a stated covenant) to add value to their group experience by extending the boundaries of their vulnerability to each other in certain ways. Finally a group becomes a team focused upon achieving a particular goal and each member agrees to endure a certain degree of conflict and mutual criticism (or accountability) in their group relationships in order to achieve this goal. (For more details see *Holy Places, Small Spaces* DR 2004 pp. 101-107.)

Church leaders are often encouraged to add as many "open chair" type classes as they can in order to grow the nurturing segment of the congregation. The logic is pretty easy to grasp. A new class is started and six people enroll. The leader puts an empty seventh chair in the circle and says, "Lets all pray together that someone will join us here next week." Several of the members agree to invite their acquaintances and week-by-week, the little circle grows. Meanwhile, the leader begins to mentor an assistant. When the room begins to feel crowded, or when the class size has reached a predetermined point (perhaps twelve), the group divides with half of the members agreeing to follow the assistant leader out and form a new class. For children and youth, this division can be based on age or gender lines.

Some churches have experienced significant statistical growth once their membership understood and affirmed the "reproductive cell" concept that underlies open chair classes and small groups. Even when one is offering a large group educational experience, such as hosting a guest lecturer for several weeks, the chances of success are significantly improved when the participants are given encouragement and specific instructions on how to invite others to participate. One church does a special Lenten Bible study and on the first week gives every attendee two attractive bookmarks that tell the times and topics of the whole study. Participants are then instructed to give the second marker away to a friend and to pray for that person during the next forty days.

Most churches need both open chair and covenantal groups to meet the needs of members and to experience healthy growth. At some point in their lives, most people feel a need to be part of a group in which they can both feel safe and be encouraged to be vulnerable. The need for deeper community is a significant motivation that churches that offer only open chair classes fail to capitalize upon. Lacking the option to participate in a covenant discipleship small group, many church members will unconsciously sabotage their Sunday school class so that new members don't arrive and interrupt the security the group feels with each other. The decline in small group participation, experienced by many churches, may have two related causes:

- First, the failure to clearly designate every class as either an open chair group or as a closed membership covenant style group.

- Second, the failure to create a sufficient number and variety of discipleship formation groups with stated covenants of accountability and vulnerability for their participants.

In failing to be intentional about our nurturing structure, we have neither encouraged people to be inviting, nor have we provided them with safe places to get to know each other on a deeper level.

Conflict in Worship

Worship can either be structured to provide sanctuary away from the conflict of daily life, or it can be structured to invite the conflict of our mundane world onto holy ground and provide catharsis and new insights that worshipers can take home with them. Churches vary in terms of how they balance these two opposing goals for worship, and every service is in some sense a compromise. I sometimes wonder if church marquees shouldn't carry a rating beside their worship times to warn visitors of their dramatic content:

G   – This service will be good for everyone. You will be invited to leave your cares at home and simply relax.

PG — This service will praise God for the good things and only make vague references to those areas of life where you may be experiencing conflict.

R — This is service is seeking real religion. You will be invited to bring all of your troubles here and lay them on the altar.

X — This service may be too extreme for most Christians. You will be challenged to consider how God relates to every aspect of your life and be expected to display your emotions freely when the service hits a nerve.

NR — This service is not rated. No one has thought intentionally about how to design it for conflict or the pastor and church leadership are in a disagreement about how it is to be structured.

The same rules that apply to small groups also apply to worship with regard to conflict. Every church worship service is a play within a play. Each week, some things are done that mimic the tensions we experience as we live out our faith in the world. One must bear in mind that conflict is related to energy in a book or play as well as in a worship service. Without conflict, there is no plot. If conflict is mishandled or allowed to exist without boundaries or structure, we put down the book, exit the theater, or leave the congregation. How much conflict we permit in our voluntary activities is both a matter of personal taste and of the skill employed by the author, director, or worship committee. Many church leaders desire to bring the energy level of their worship service up a notch, but the path of least resistance and minimal effort usually results in a bland "G" or "PG" rating.

Consider the following:

- When the scriptures are read, the worship is structured so that people are invited to empathize and identify with the biblical characters. This might be done through the use of drama or dramatic readings, visual arts, dance, or interpretive movement. Be intentionally about selecting music to mirror the emotional content of the scriptures.

- People feel comfortable sharing their deeper needs during prayer time. Time must be set aside for requests to be offered by those who may be hesitant in speech. Worship leaders need to be intentional about the phrases they use to encourage the degree of vulnerability the worship team is seeking at this point in the service. People might be offered a variety of ways of submitting their prayer concerns, so that they can place their needs on a slip of paper, move to a place at the altar, or have someone else speak for them, depending upon their comfort level.

- Joys, testimonies, and praise elements of the service are separated from the time of prayer concerns, so that people are not required to repeatedly oscillate between rejoicing with those who rejoice and weeping with those who weep.

- The person who brings the message is clear as to whether the sermon will comfort the afflicted or afflict the comfortable. The sermon structure and illustrations are chosen to achieve this intent. If teaching points in the sermon will help people, list these points in the bulletin.

Worship teams can alter congregational custom and practice for a variety of reasons. Energy, vulnerability, and conflict can be designed into or out of any given style of worship. I visit a variety of churches and I have found it increasingly difficult to predict the level of energy I will experience. In one place, a church's physical structure may be daunting, its denomination traditional, and its location depressing, but I find a congregation fully engaged in a dramatic experience as they see their troubles and joys translated into liturgy. In a more upscale congregation, led by a non-denominational pastor and one that ministers to younger people, I have experienced a lack of plot: worship contained nothing to make me feel that my life has been addressed or to give me a reason to return.

Bad Conflict

Since nurturing structures make use of personal conflict to transform and heal the lives of their participants, they need to be perceived as "safe" places. Individuals generally do not participate in a class or attend a worship service because they enjoy the energy of church conflict. Parents do not send their children to a youth group in hopes that the children will be pawns in the power struggle between the church board and their group leader. Instead, it is in the very nature of a nurturing group that it can only function well when it is isolated from institutional conflict and able to provide a safe place for individuals to learn about their own issues. This fundamental principle means that certain rules must be adopted for both the classroom and the sanctuary:

- Those who come in contact with youth, children, and the disabled must have the necessary clearances and training. One of the structures that every church, regardless of size, must develop is a set of policies and procedures to protect those in our care from the possible abuse. (See *Safe Sanctuaries*, by Joy Thornburg Melton, Discipleship Resources.)

- Children's classrooms and the nursery must be clean, well maintained, and regularly inspected for potential hazards. These learning areas must be perceived as safe places.

- Christian education staff, volunteers, and others must be able to work within the church administrative system. Develop clear guidelines for supervision, including a grievance policy and process.

- Those who preach must be careful not to use their message time to win support for their side of a church conflict or to garner votes for an upcoming administrative meeting. Worship as nurture is best supported when leaders establish a protective boundary around these sacred hours of the week. The pulpit can and should be used to address issues of social justice, to prick the moral conscience of the congregation, and to wade into theological understandings of the nature of the church and the kingdom of God. When it is used to voice the pastor's side of petty issues or to chastise the specific faults of persons in the congregation, the role that worship plays in helping the congregation to express and grow in the their love of God and neighbor is put in serious jeopardy.

Models for Nurturing Structures

If you survey church life in America, you will discover a confusing variety of approaches to nurture. One church may have a designated Sunday school hour in which people attend age appropriate classes to grasp the intellectual side of the faith, followed by a worship service that engages the heart through ritual, music, and participation in the sacraments. Other churches place an extended message or "teaching time" at the heart of the worship service for adults and offer a similar worship/teaching experience for children at the same hour in a different part of the building. Still other churches are very fluid, allowing worship and education to flow back and forth in every setting. Some churches only offer Christian education in age or gender segregated classes, which meet in the building at designated times. Other churches experiment freely with intergenerational classes, home Bible study, and short-term educational events.

Nurture structures are functional, not when they follow the latest fad, but when they significantly help people to love the Lord. This should be the deciding factor in adopting or altering various structures. Church leaders should be careful about designing or choosing nurture programs. The existing nurture structure of your church is built upon an underlying sense of congregational identity. Today, there are two models for nurture that strive for adoption by the church. Many church leaders are attempting to mix incompatible elements from these opposing understandings about nurture. While in practice, blended worship and "mix and match" Christian education is working for many congregations, I think it important for church leaders to be aware of how fundamentally opposed these two approaches are.

THE TRADITIONAL MODEL

Most congregations have a proven form of worship that they simply seek to perform faithfully, with quality and integrity, each week. To be successful in the traditional method of nurture, a congregation must devote time and resources training children and youth in the meaning of this traditional form of worship. These formative practices build upon the significance of the Christian calendar, the meaning of the sacraments, and the liturgical responses of the people during worship. Worship and Christian education are inseparable partners in the task of conveying the traditions of the church from one generation to the next. Churches that do the traditional method of nurture well are unapologetic about their attachment to historic creeds and tested forms of worship. Having tasted the old wine and found it to be fulfilling, they are committed to traditional structures for worship, prayer, and the instruction of new members (Luke 5:39).

THE CONTEMPORARY MODEL

From time to time church leaders discover anew that the love of God is communicated outside of the traditional structures. They experiment with new forms of worship. They meet for study and prayer in homes and neighborhood coffee shops. For them, worship and small groups are inseparable partners in the task of helping everyday people experience and know God. The nuts and bolts of the worship service, the history of the church, and the roles of various religious leaders are subjects rarely discussed in these study groups. The purpose of gathering is to explore together the relevance of Christian faith for the contemporary world. The community gathers at convenient times and locations. They adopt flexible structures for nurture, judging each change on how well it enables people to support each other in their experience of God. Having been filled with new wine, the contemporary congregation bursts any remaining traditional structures and forms new ones (Luke 5:37).

I offer the above two paragraphs to counteract the misconception that shifting to contemporary worship is merely a matter of changing the music, adding a LCD projector to flash the words on a screen, and deciding to encourage casual attire. In the contemporary model there is a fundamental shift from the understanding of a traditional congregation. For the congregation with a traditional sense of identity, the form of its worship is part of the religious content that it hopes to transmit to the next generation. For the contemporary congregation, the form of its worship is a pragmatic, week-by-week decision. With this in mind, I offer the following personal observations:

- Contemporary and traditional models are equally valid and sustainable in today's world.

- The religious marketplace of most American communities has room for a limited number of purely traditional congregations. It is rare, however, to find a community that is saturated with contemporary congregations.

- When a traditional congregation decides to add a contemporary worship service, they should recognize that they are birthing another congregation. This new child will share resources and compete for the attention of leadership, but in the end must enjoy freedom to discover its own identity.

- When contemporary and traditional congregations share the same church building, the shared leadership needs to allocate worship times on the basis of what will be most effective in helping those currently outside the church find a home in the church. This usually means having traditional worship early on Sunday and Contemporary worship on Saturday evenings and in the Sunday morning "prime time."

- It is easier for a church to have three or more worship services than it is to have one or two. Having only one service gives people a "take it or leave it" choice that lacks the flexibility most families want today. Two worship services can be polarizing, even if they are both the same style, because the congregations are pitted against each other for resources, meeting times, and leadership.

Nurture Structures in Contemporary Culture

We need to add to these specific observations the more general fact that today's culture has become highly intolerant of inconvenient nurture. Having to live in a cramped dorm room was once gladly accepted as the entry fee for a college education. Today's perspective student expects their school living quarters to have room to entertain and many other conveniences. This emphasis on convenience is interlaced with the general expectation that people be life-long learners. Going away to college is no longer viewed as a once in a lifetime "boot camp" type experience. Now, people expect their academic environment will be homelike. Taking this trend one step further, many people today take classes online or engage in distance learning.

These trends change what people expect from worship and Christian education. People will not send their children into a dingy basement room for an hour of religious indoctrination. Instead, they expect the church to nurture their children into loving the Lord for life. Colorful environments and experiential learning has become the norm. Children are given an interactive lesson, which may include drama or peer-to-peer learning and then told to look up the day's Bible lesson online for further research. Adults are open to some of the same techniques, but their real shift has come in terms of what they expect in worship. They want their congregational experience to be warm and familiar, as well as interesting and relevant, because they plan to invest in it as an integrated part of their lives. They are no longer willing to sit in a cold pew and hear a lecture. They want to participate in something that will help them to love the Lord more. This can be traditional or contemporary in its paradigm, but it must be relevant to the task of loving God today.

The Church Calendar

The primary structure used by a congregation to provide worship and Christian education for its people is the church calendar. Just as the first chapter of Genesis delights in showing how God brought order out of darkness and chaos by announcing the sacred sequence of a week ending with a Sabbath, so the story of the church is one of visionary leaders providing structures of gathering and ritual in the midst of a people who lack the discipline to order their daily lives in a godly way. The church calendar needs to be prayerfully designed. *When* we do something is often more important than *what* we do. Insightful church leaders make frequent attempts to gather information on the congregation's lifestyle and availability. If, for example, congregational members are primarily retired and living on fixed incomes, planning an event with a cost on the third weekend of the month may be a bad idea. Most congregations have discovered that the school calendar influences attendance and leadership availability for certain events, but few congregations have gone the next step to plan their calendars around the rhythms of modern life.

For example, the annual church meeting (in the United Methodist Church the Charge or Church Conference, 2004 Discipline par.244-246) should be held in May. The season that runs from the day after Easter until the beginning of August is a natural time of transition for our Western culture. Holding the annual meeting in the midst of this time permits communication to focus on how the church is changing. The spiritual boost that accompanies the end of Lent should be harvested for missional ideas and new goals. The importance of spiritual leadership is reinforced by the story of Pentecost that marks this season. New leaders take office in the early summer, so they are fully onboard, mentored, and enthusiastic about the new fall season.

Most churches continue the old agrarian model of scheduling the annual meeting in the fall, just after the harvest. When all of our members were farmers, this made sense because the lengthening nights brought downtime for folk to be gathered in for a long meeting. Today, fall is an extremely busy time for families as well as for those whose work caters to the needs of younger Americans. It packs three major shopping holidays (yes, I include Halloween), an urgent list of "must-see" TV, the drama of football and politics, and the mayhem of new school classes. Fall is a critical time for the church to engage culture. Church leaders need to focus on ministry and outreach as they enter the Labor Day through Christmas rush.

Packrat Structures

The things we do for nurture accumulate structure. A group within the church, for example, may have a brief dedication service for their officers and work as they begin a new year. The first year, someone stands up and offers a brief prayer. The second year, the service includes two passages of scripture, a litany, and a prayer. The third year, the service grows to include lighting candles, singing hymns, and taking an offering. Soon the service will include a guest speaker, a budget line, and a planning committee. This is a great blessing if it helps the participants to grow in their love of God.

Perhaps more than any of the other functional structures discussed in this book, nurture is the place where less is better. In worship, care must be taken not to let the accretions of announcements, special offerings, litanies, and special music crowd out the sacred. People lose interest when they are confused or receive too much information. Having something different every ninety seconds does not keep people interested in worship; it distracts them. Classes and small groups need to remain well defined and simple in their format to be effective. Some of the adult education offerings should to be short-term electives. Classes and groups need to be dropped, weeded out, and reconstituted on a regular basis. Only by being scrupulous can we rise above the clutter of accumulated "used to be good" programs and really do the task of nurturing the faith of today's congregation.

CHAPTER FOUR

Equip: Where People Are Empowered To Be Jesus' Disciples

Test for Stone Three: Does Jan Get the Job?

Imagine that two years have gone by since the waitress Jan first showed up for worship in your church. You know her as a hard-working single parent with a big heart and with limited time for church work. When helping to clean up after a church dinner, Jan noticed that something was wrong in the church kitchen. Having worked in restaurants, she knows how a busy kitchen should be arranged. She also knows the state and local codes for food safety. She wants to know how to change the layout and procedures of your church kitchen.

This test invites you to think about how your congregation receives people who have a limited religious background. Jan may have been inside a church a dozen times before landing in your church. Something about your church has captured her heart and now she attends worship when her work schedule permits. Since your church is a very nurturing place, Jan is also a member of a small group in church. Her classmates know her as a sincere person who does not know the local church procedures or the rules of your denomination. She seems unsure of how to relate to your pastor. Does your church value her naiveté?

1) Given Jan's limited time availability and irregular schedule, which meaningful church positions and service opportunities would be available to her? List those that you think a person like Jan would be asked to consider and score half a point for each, up to five total points.

2) Does your church value new attendees and intentionally place them on planning committees so that the church organization can be given new ways of seeing things?

    __ Never has in the past. = -1

    __ The pastor or another significant church leader will occasionally ask new attendees to serve, if they personally like them. = 0

    __ Your lay leadership committee (nominations) considers new attendees to be equally qualified for most church positions. = 1

    __ Some positions are intentionally set aside for new attendees so that their outsider's perspective can be heard. = 2

3) Does your church have well reasoned expectations for those in leadership positions that involve decision making for the congregation (Church Council, Trustees, and so forth)? Expectations may include attendance at worship, stewardship, supporting the other members of the team in prayer, etc.

    __ No = 0   __ Yes = 2

4) How well does the church office function in supporting the work of all church leaders? (One point for each positive answer.)

    __ Basic office equipment is labeled and well supplied, so leaders can make quick adjustments and copies to their class notes, meeting agendas, and so forth.

___ Internet access is available in the church.

___ The secretary's role involves service to all leaders, not just the pastor.

___ The church calendar is kept current and located where it can be viewed by those attending evening meetings.

___ (Add an additional point if the church calendar is also maintained on the church website.)

___ Church leaders are informed by email and phone messages from the church office regarding changes in meeting location, time, or agenda.

5) The housing allowance or parsonage provided for the clergy is evaluated each year with an eye towards the incentive it provides for quality leadership to serve the congregation. If you are providing a parsonage, consider the following:

- Does it provide privacy for the pastor's family?

- Does it meet all of your denominational parsonage standards?

- Is it maintained and modified in a way that accommodates the tastes and needs of the current parsonage family?

- Does the parsonage size or accessibility affect the availability of pastors willing to serve the congregation?

If you are providing a housing allowance, reflect upon whether your congregation is willing to be served by a pastor who lives outside of your area. Are you willing to provide more money in travel allowance if it reduces the amount needed for housing?

Score between 0 to four points after reflecting upon the above. _____
Score for Stone Three: _____

This test has a possible score of twenty, which can be multiplied times five to give you a recognizable grade; 90-100 "Excellent", 80-89 "Good, but room for improvement," 70-79 "passing", 60 and below "You are failing to empower people to be disciples." The score on this stone should be compared with the other tests to give your leadership a sense as to which structures are functional and which ones don't fit the mission your church has in the world.

Empowering People to be Jesus' Disciples

An army of a thousand is easy to find, but, ah,
how difficult to find a general.

Chinese Proverb

According to the Greek myth, Zeus had a headache. Unable to rid himself of the headache, Zeus asked his friend Prometheus to take a whack at his head with an ax. Out of Zeus' broken skull a fully-grown woman emerged. The woman, Athena, became his favorite daughter. Not only did she spare him all the tasks of parenting and ease his headache, but she also arrived fully equipped to help out with Olympian tasks. Athena was born wise, beautiful, and wearing battle armor. This method for producing leaders has been tried over and over in the church and has yet to work for us like it did for Zeus.

Finding good leaders in the church sometimes seems like a harsh headache. The most common methods for producing and placing church leaders make as much sense as Zeus' Promethean aspirin. They include:

- Hoping that our leaders will transfer from another congregation;

- Dropping people into tasks without training them;

- Making membership the only requirement for lay leadership;

- Making ordination the only requirement for pastoral leadership;

- Encouraging autonomous activity instead of teamwork;

- Using the democratic process (voting) instead of prayerful discernment;

- Requiring or allowing people to remain in the same job forever;

- Honoring people for the positions they hold rather than the spiritual gifts that bring;

- Expecting leaders to solve problems;

- Not allowing people to fail, forget, or honor their non-church commitments.

This list may seem strange and counterintuitive, but these methods relate to our hope that leaders will show up fully equipped to do battle like Athena. The church needs structures to be in place that empower people to be disciples. We need to be able to guide a person step-by-step from initial commitment to Christ to move in the journey toward Christian maturity. The goal of your congregation's leadership structure should be the full empowering of every person who participates. It has to work for the person who grows up in the church as well as the person who arrives at midlife.

Farm Teams

Most professional sports teams pay close attention to their process for leadership development, both for their players and their coaches. Baseball uses a farm team system. Instead of simply filling the nine positions on the field, they actively sponsor a number of minor league teams in graded levels. Professional football casts an even larger recruitment net by drawing its players up from college and high school teams. Skills are taught at these lower levels and the players are instilled with a sense of team culture.

In the church, we are constantly recruiting people to tasks that rarely occur in the secular world. Before Sam came to our church, he did not know how to sing with a choir, load a hundred-cup coffee maker, or help serve communion. The welcoming quality of a congregation is not only

seen in the ways it gets people into the church, but also by how patiently
they guide newcomers into church work. A person is not fully assimi-
lated until he or she has a job to do or has joined a team. Every time a
church leader says it is easier to do a task than teach or recruit someone
else, that leader is putting a roadblock in the natural process of empowering all people to be disciples of Christ. Many old-time church folk
secretly enjoy hoarding for themselves all the simple but mysterious jobs
of the church. This is why, for example, simple instructions for using the
big coffee pot are not placed on the wall near where it is stored. Every
congregation needs to make a list of easy, short-term tasks set apart for
novice church attenders. Every congregation needs to make mentoring or
teaching others a component of every job description.

The concept here is to make the threshold for entry into church life
as low as possible. The congregational culture has to value people exactly
where they are when they come through the door. The people who come
to us are not like Athena, wise, beautiful, and fully equipped to head up
next week's vacation Bible school. They will be like Jan, whose only experience of Christian education was one week at camp when she was a
third grader. We need to set apart entry-level tasks and respect the time
limitations of each person.

At the same time, each congregation needs to establish a higher level
of values and standards for its leadership. Those groups that make decisions that impact the ministry of the church and the allocation of the
congregation's resources should develop shared expectations about what
it means to be in leadership together. The finance committee may
develop an accountability covenant that says they agree to attend worship regularly, tithe, and pray for one another each day. Groups may
agree to hold each other accountable for learning particular skills or
attending training events. The mission committee may assign each member to the task of keeping current on a particular mission field. There
may be a basic level of leadership standards that the church council will
adopt for all church leaders with the expectation that each group forms
a covenant of specific items that will be beneficial to the spiritual growth
of the participants. In order for the church to continuously improve,

there needs to be commitment on the part of leaders to strive towards personal excellence in specific ways.

Not Membership, But Discipleship!

Most churches have clear expectations surrounding membership. They have a process for joining the church and forms for transferring membership from one church to another. Membership is well structured. Unfortunately, this emphasis is both unbiblical and counter productive. I do not see any correlation between membership structures and congregational vitality. Every church needs to develop is a process for discipleship formation. Each person who tentatively begins to attend a congregation's activities needs to be encouraged, guided, and equipped until they become a fully committed disciple living out his or her faith in ways that will transform the world for Jesus Christ. Church membership is one small step somewhere in the middle of this long process.

A functional discipleship formation structure does three things well:

- First, it rapidly involves new church attendees in both the fellowship and the outreach of the church. Many people today drift from church to church looking for a place where they will be given a chance to make a difference in the world. Churches need to offer new attenders real opportunities for service.

- Second, the viewpoints and concerns of newcomers to the faith are appreciated and intentionally mined for insights as to how to make the church more receptive to other unchurched people. Churches with a good discipleship formation structure rapidly assimilate new people into the church planning process. Further, the nurturing structure of the church should be designed to help people understand and utilize their spiritual gifts and personal temperaments.

- Third, the congregation understands the goal is the full spiritual formation of every participant. The structure is designed to keep people striving to become more and more complete in their discipleship to Christ. The Wesleyan word "sanctification" may not always be verbalized in this context, but the church culture continuously expresses the desire for its people to use their spiritual gifts, live generous and transformative lives, and become more holy.

Ordination Is Not the Top Rung

A layperson in leadership at a dysfunctional church once said, "We pay our preachers to be holy so we don't have to be." He spoke in a serious tone of voice. Too often the nurturing teamwork of a church is hamstrung by an unhealthy clergy-laity relationship. Christians do not come in two distinct types, nor does becoming ordained make a person more holy. Clergy need to coach and support the various nurture-related groups and ministries of the church. They should not be the source of all of a church's worship ideas, formative theology, or spiritual growth programs. Often, clergy who have a more private or scholastic understanding of their own faith will inadvertently lower the nurturing climate of a congregation by making spiritual growth appear to be something too abstract or complex for the lay person. On the other hand, clergy who are extraverted in their spirituality will often overshadow the insights and contributions of the laity. This not only leaves the congregation at a loss when that pastor moves; it limits the spiritual depth that the laity will strive to obtain.

The goal of all nurturing structures is to help people grow in their love for God. For most individuals this process leads them not to ordination, but to more fruitful service and deeper holiness as believers. We do not judge the effectiveness of a congregation by the number of young people sent to seminary, but by the breadth of commitment to a Christian lifestyle found in its average member. To this end, pastors need to intentionally coach others in spiritual formation. They need to model personal integrity and become transparent about their spiritual goals and struggles. They will want to train others to lead Bible studies and small groups so these areas of church life can replicate without being limited by needing pastoral oversight. Pastors will want to spread the leadership and creative input for worship out to a trusted team of laity. Team leadership of worship is one of the leading early indicators of church vitality. Congregational growth is often linked to worship teams who pray together, hold each other accountable for quality work week after week, and evaluate each element of worship, including sermon and choral anthems.

Clergy Housing

Congregations are often unaware that the system of clergy housing is dysfunctional. One church may provide a beautiful Victorian home with cavernous rooms to a single pastor with modest tastes. Meanwhile, another church squeezes its clergy family of five into a cramped parsonage, while converting the backyard of the home into parking or a play area for the church-run daycare. A third congregation provides a housing allowance, but restricts that housing allowance to an expensive neighborhood near the church.

I am going to go out on a limb and say three things that many denominational officials are afraid to say:

- Clergy housing is a form of clergy compensation. Few things are as deeply personalized and cherished in the American psyche as the choices we make about where we live. If a church provides a parsonage, it not only has to keep the house attractive and livable, it has to insure that there aren't any aspects of the property that will limit the quality of future pastoral leadership. Churches need to evaluate their housing annually.

- Clergy families need privacy. Church-owned houses that are near the church may reinforce an unhealthy codependency between the congregation and its pastor.

- Parsonages, especially those that are adjacent to the church building, can often be better utilized in other ways. Sometimes a parsonage sits on the only property available to improve parking. Releasing control of clergy housing may free the congregation to do some new creative form of mission outreach.

The Church Office and Other Common Rooms

The church office needs to be viewed as a resource that supports the work of all leaders, especially those involved in nurture. Unfortunately, many churches view the church administrative assistant's role as primarily one to support the pastor. In today's computer enabled society the average church leader may not need the traditional typing and filing functions to support their work, but they still need a one-stop place for obtaining and distributing information. The physical church office needs to compliment and parallel the Internet virtual office. Small membership churches may dispense with an actual church office and simply maintain a copier, computer, worktable, mailboxes, and filing cabinet for use by all leaders.

The key is to make the tools of communication accessible to all those who need it. Update the church calendar continuously and have it available online and in church meeting sites. Setting up a wireless Internet network is relatively simple, and such access helps teachers and leaders. Keep a photocopier in a safe and unlocked space. Many models now come with capability to add security codes.

The more flexible the church's physical space, the better the church will nurture others. Avoid letting one adult class or group tie up and "own" a room. When one group has a proprietary claim on the parlor, then other groups will not fully utilize this space. Shuffling classrooms so the larger groups have the better rooms keeps "open chair" groups seeking more members. Do not let tradition distract us from the task of helping people love the Lord.

CHAPTER FIVE

Envision: When Committees Really Work

Test for Stone Four: Is It Easy to Get Things Done?

Take this test for each of the committees on which you serve. Key committees in the church may wish to set aside a meeting to take the test and discuss their results. How does your personal aggravation rating compare with the others around the table? If you participate in or look at the results from several committees, are there any common elements? Should your whole organization seek to learn a new pattern for conducting its business? This test seeks to illuminate the sticking points within your decision-making structure.

1) Self-Awareness: Does each member of the committee know what the committee is responsible for? Are the tasks and procedures of the group well explained to those who are new to it? Does the work of this committee fit neatly together with the work of others in the church?

Yes . . . . No

How aggravating is the lack of self-awareness for this committees work?

Very aggravating .... Neutral .... Not a problem

2) Meeting Times and Attendance: Are the meetings held at times and days of the week that are convenient for all members? Do you seek to have 100% attendance at your meetings?

Yes . . . . No

How aggravating is the low attendance for this committees work?

Very aggravating .... Neutral .... Not a problem

3) Goals and Objectives: Are the goal and objectives of this committee talked about? Is sufficient time devoted towards developing a strategy to improve this area of church life? Is the work of this committee set within the context of overall goal(s) of the congregation?

Yes . . . . No

How aggravating is the lack of strategic planning for this committees work?

Very aggravating .... Neutral .... Not a problem

4) Follow-through and Performance: Do the meetings end with the clear assignment of various tasks for members to do before the next meeting? Is there follow-up on decisions that are made? Are the minutes or decisions available for the members and others to review between meetings?

Yes . . . . No

How aggravating is the lack of follow-through for this committees work?

Very aggravating .... Neutral .... Not a problem

Overall Aggravation Score: How would you judge the effectiveness of this committee?

D...............C...............B...............A

Very aggravating .... Neutral .... Not a problem

Committees That Really Work

Speech is conveniently located midway between thought and action,
where it often substitutes for both.

John Andrew Holmes

"Come, let us build ourselves a city, with a tower that reaches to the
heavens, so that we may make a name for ourselves and not be scat-
tered over the face of the whole earth." But the LORD came down to
see the city and the tower that the men were building.
The LORD said, "If as one people speaking the same language they
have begun to do this, then nothing they plan to do will be impossible
for them. Come, let us go down and confuse their language so they
will not understand each other."

Genesis 11:4-7

"Well, there goes the neighborhood."

Anonymous bystander at the Tower of Babel building project

The Tower of Babel story begins with a people who seek to build a
structure that will give their community a focal point. "We need to make
a name for ourselves," was their cry (Genesis 11:4). So they formed a
building committee and all went well for a while. Some of human history's most painful failures have involved people looking to structures
for their sense of identity. In South Africa, apartheid was a structure of
racial segregation imposed to provide a national identity for the white
minority. My own city recently built two sports stadiums and is contem-
plating a third as well as a gambling casino, not because the town's teams
lack a place to play, but because the political leaders want to create a new
identity for the city as an entertainment hot spot. A structure may
indeed provide us with a name for ourselves; but how does that name
relate to our humanity or the mission we have from God?

This may be why the Bible uses the story of the Tower of Babel as the preface for the narrative of Abraham's walk with God. Abraham travels away from a culture of building towers to live in a tent without a city to call his own. His journey seems designed to provide God with a blank slate on which to write a new identity. The children of Abraham become known for their capacity to bless, rather than for their structures (Genesis 12:2-3). Some congregations today are known for the building they meet in, while others are known for the ministries they do. One of the fundamental tasks of leadership is to help committees understand how structures, congregational identity, and mission in this particular context all interrelate.

Every committee needs to know how their tasks and areas of oversight fit within the larger structure of the church. They also need to discuss how the congregation's identity is enhanced by their committee work. Further, they need to know the overall mission of the church and any short-term goals the church council has adapted. The committee structure, meeting times, membership, and agenda need constant monitoring to ensure its fit within the congregation. For example, if the mission and identity of the congregation involves integrating the church program with the students and faculty of the neighboring college, then the membership of many committees will need to be intentionally chosen to include college people. The structure of these committees may be improved by following the local academic calendar. Structure the organization of the church around the people who fit your identity, mission, and ministry.

Communication

In Christian theology, Pentecost is the "un-tower-of-Babel" story. In the second chapter of Acts the curse of being unable to communicate and work together was removed amidst a flurry of heavenly tongues and celestial fire. Pentecost released the early church to work across cultures and generations to build the kingdom of God. The heart of this new kingdom is a shared sense of identification with Christ. Strangers are able, by God's Spirit, to partner together for a greater good. Old roles, such as master and slave or Greek and Jew, are no longer points of division among the disciples of Christ.

Every time people lose sight of the church's mission, they draw the entire organization back to that ancient plain of Shinar and the tower. When people suspect their committee's task is trivial or lacks connection to the purpose God has for the church, they say and do silly things. The committee may be led by a chair who knows parliamentary procedure, and yet they find themselves bogged down in minutia or rearranging the agenda and tabling motions. Committee members arrive late and leave early, and failure to prepare becomes acceptable behavior for all members. When the work of a committee exceeds or moves in another direction from the mission and goals of the congregation, communication fails in other ways. The group may be dominated by a few voices or become secretive and defensive about its actions. Little effort is made to integrate what this committee is doing with the overall work of the church. The congregation is divided into insiders and outsiders: those who know why we are building a tower and those who don't.

Looking back to the early chapter of Acts, one notes how Christ's statement of his mission for the early church is only separated by ten days from the manifestation of the Holy Spirit at Pentecost (Acts 1:8; 2:1-47). There is a profound relationship between the clarity with which a group understands how its tasks line up with the purposes of God and the grace they receive to perform those tasks. The people of Babel did not get sidetracked into building the foolish tower when their leadership ignored standard operating procedure. The tower of Babel project arose, like many of the projects we become involve with, out of a failure to be mindful of what God wants the organization to do in its particular context. The decision-making structure you adopt for your church is the vital link between envisioning the will of God and doing it in your context.

Poor Choices

The story of the tower of Babel is also one of cheap counterfeits and poor choices. The people use brick for stones and tar for mortar. They also organize themselves around the task of building of a stairway to heaven rather than seeking to discover a meaningful relationship with God. In the church, being active is often a substitute for being holy.

Having a committee on evangelism is a substitute for witnessing to our faith. Doing a mission fair is a substitute for being active participants in outreach work. Spending a weekend in fellowship, games, and endless hours rearranging the wording of the church mission statement is often a poor substitute for a substantial yearly planning retreat.

The end result is that our meetings are boring. One of the chief reasons for this is our failure to manage productive conflict when it appears in our meetings. When an issue is worth addressing, people will naturally speak with more passion. They will step on toes and state truths that church leaders has been avoiding if they feel their free speech will lead to change. Often, a committee chair will squash disagreement for fear that a contentious meeting will reflect badly on his or her leadership. Nurturing passionate speech in committees requires courage. It also requires constant attention to the mission and identity of the congregation, so that when people argue, they do so to advance a common cause, rather than out of petty jealousy.

I highly recommend that church leaders read *The Five Dysfunctions of a Team* by Patrick Lencioni (Jossey-Bass, 2002). This short business book deals with how to develop teams and committees into groups that hold each other accountable for their shared efforts. Today, we rarely criticize committee members who come to the meeting unprepared to debate the issues that are on the agenda. We fail to allow sufficient time and research to empower leaders to think strategically. Our meetings rarely begin with a quick check of how each member carried out their tasks from past meetings, and they rarely end with a commitment on the part of each member to follow up in specific ways. These failures do not arise from the lack of spirituality, intelligence, or Christian commitment. Rather, they are the result of poor team development. When people are grouped together to make decisions or to oversee an area of congregational life, they need to develop a certain level of trust in each other as team players. They need to step off of this foundation and risk vulnerability and conflict in their group relationships. The group needs to be guided over the course of a year towards progressively higher levels of commitment and accountability for their shared tasks. The committee leader then has a dual task: to make the group "gel" (relate intensely and intentionally with each other) and to keep the focus of the committee upon results.

Types of Church Meetings

The decisions that committees make and the discussions that occupy their time fall into two distinct categories:

- **Actions.** This category includes discussion of policies, dates, expenditures, and responses to short term issues. Committees act, often by providing permission and resources for others to do their work, out of a previously adopted understanding of the church's identity and mission.

- **Visions.** Every committee needs to devote time to understanding how its particular scope and tasks relate to the short-term goals of the church, the congregation's sense of identity, and their mission to make disciples for Christ in this particular context. Continuous assessment of current reality will lead to visionary strategy and ever-changing tactics for a constant improvement of the church's witness and service.

Individuals have a hard time adjusting to discussions that bounce back and forth between the active and the visionary. Committees bog down and fail to complete tasks when talk about specific actions becomes interrupted by general concerns about the church. People feel bored when they become confused by a shift in topic or led onto an irrelevant tangent. Boring meetings reduce the level of passion for critical issues, lower member attendance, and increase the time needed to complete simple tasks.

The answer is to stick inflexibly to the agenda, but to plan for two different types of meetings: "action meetings" and "vision meetings." A committee that meets every month may designate one meeting per quarter as a vision meeting. The agenda of this meeting will focus on "big picture" issues. This is the time to develop priorities and break major objectives into step-by-step projects. It will also be the time to assign research tasks for those issues the committee has a hard time resolving, such as new forms or services of worship or new types of ministry.

Churches, regardless of their size, should invest in an effective yearly planning retreat. This becomes the "vision meeting" for everyone. During the yearly retreat, the whole leadership sets the short-term objective(s) of the church for the coming year. Each church leader has the opportunity to see how the committee's work fits into the larger work of the whole congregation. The energy needed to improve each of the church's structures is discovered. The common language and energy of Pentecost is often experienced in these events. Leaders from differing aspects of the church life return with a renewed commitment to support one another in prayer and to hold their committees accountable for their part of the congregation's shared vision.

Valuing People's Time

For the organizational structure of a church to work, the whole church must appreciate the time people donate to leadership tasks. Many fine Christian leaders may be unable to serve in such roles because their work prevents them from participating in a committee that meets from 7:00 to 9:30 pm on the third Monday of the month. They may do shift-work, be single parents, or no longer drive at night. More than ever, the work of the church needs to be distributed into a variety of time slots. Splitting traditional committees into small single-task teams of two or three people allows meetings to take place in people's homes at their convenience. Modern technology allows decisions to be made via conference call or over the Internet. Agile church leaders tailor the work that needs to be done to the time that people are able to commit. The church can no longer afford to make people feel guilty because they cannot commit to the traditional, inflexible meeting times.

When I need to call together a group of busy people, I often pass around a sheet of paper (or circulate an email) listing a number of possible meeting dates and times. I ask each to initial the dates they cannot meet. The date and times that remain are the ones we plan into our schedule. In this way I express my appreciation for the fact that people have commitments beyond this particular church committee. I couple this with a request that they send advance notification when circumstances make it impossible for them to attend a meeting. If the committee is small or the contribution of the individual is critical, I have no problems rescheduling a meeting at the last moment. In this way I hope to develop a culture in the committee that values 100% attendance. Having a high rate of attendance allows committees to be smaller and to meet less frequently.

Each committee will develop its own culture, which will determine its ideal meeting duration and format. Some committees need to do a certain amount of relational "checking in" before business. Other committees function best when they are confined to a narrow time frame. A mission committee may meet at the local diner from 6:00 am to 7:00 am every other Tuesday before people go to work. This puts them in a pray, eat, and handle one item of business mode of operation. Trustees may function best as two separate teams, one meeting during the day and doing a lot of "walk around" property management, while another meets at night and focuses on paperwork and budget figures. The two teams meet together every other month or once a quarter to make official decisions. The concept calls for the current committee members to determine the schedule and the agenda, rather than to be stuck to tradition or precedent.

Decision-making committees should be small. When there are fifteen or more people filling a room, it is easy to doubt the significance of your particular contribution. When you share a small table with a half dozen others, the sacrifice to be there is more likely to be justified. Small groups reach the level of trust where they can experience constructive conflict and hold each other accountable for results quicker than large groups.

Task Force Rules

Many people are only able to make short-term commitments—whether to a project or a small-group study. Some committees burn out church workers because the committee process squandered time or imposed all of the work upon the few. The best way to reactivate the disillusioned or capture those who have never held a church position is to create a short-term task force.

The phrase *task force* should refer only to those groups that have specific tasks and limited duration. People should know that when they agree to serve on a task force their service will end when the project is done. This frees them to commit more energy to the task, often meeting more once during a week. It also allows them to develop creative solutions that standing committees would miss. Further, task forces are free to involve people who are ineligible for regular committees. Ideal task force people may be transient (college students home on break), non-church members, and new residents to the community.

Never create a new standing committee when a task force can handle the task. Seasonal events, such as vacation Bible school or the annual church fundraiser, should not be assigned to standing committees. Instead, a few leaders should convene as many task forces as necessary to complete the task. This task force approach encourages the involvement of more people. The task force leaders continuously recruit more people until they have enough to do what needs to be done.

Leadership Rotation

Perhaps the single most important policy a church can maintain is a set of term limits. Those on the decision-making committees of a church, with the exception of church council, should rotate off those committees. When a committee has a limited number of members, such as the trustees, allowing people to serve beyond a three-year term reduces the new people appointed to that body. A person who discovers that he or she is the only one who is new to the group will be shy about asking questions and suggesting new alternatives. Even the best leaders, when they are extended beyond their term limits, reinforce the church's inherent bent towards conservative institutional preservation. It is impossible to have constructive structural change while still maintaining a culture that entrenches the old guard.

CHAPTER SIX

Send: When Giving Becomes Joyful

Test for Stone Five: Money to Mission. How Cool Is That?

1) Is giving motivated by guilt ("if we don't give, our pastor will starve") or by mission ("we give so that others will know the joy of our faith")?

0…………..2…………..3…………..4…………..5

Guilt Motivation   both   Mission Motivation

2) Does the budgeting process take place within the context of the church's overall mission and its short-term goal(s)? This means setting the budget (or ministry spending plan) after the yearly planning retreat and including a rationale for each item based on the current objectives of the church.

0…………..2…………..3…………..4…………..5

No Budget   No Planning   Strategic Budgeting

3) Are the various committees and fellowships in the church invited to think creatively about what they would do if they had additional funds? Do the people who are working on the frontlines realize how gains in total church income will get distributed into additional resources for them to do their job?

0.............2.............3.............4.............5

No Involvement   High Involvement

4) Does the church council regularly publish both the objectives they hope to achieve and the funds that each objective will require? For example, if the council decides to add a leadership retreat to this year's budget, will both the costs and the importance of that event be communicated to the congregation?

0.............2.............3.............4.............5

No Communication   Some   Constant Communication

5) Are all accounts audited each year? Are the results of the audit made available to the public?

0.............2.............3.............4.............5

No   Yes

Joyful Givers

"Suppose one of you wants to build a tower.
Will he not first sit down and estimate the cost to see if he has
enough money to complete it?

Luke 14:28

Every church needs a structure to spend money. Most churches already have structures that are good at saving or managing money, but spending money is another story. The financial structure of a congregation should not resemble a canteen, but rather a fire hydrant. A canteen is designed to carry water and dole it out one swallow at a time, whereas a fire hydrant provides access to an unlimited water supply to save life. Fire companies have special procedures for tapping into the water supply, and local ordinances curtail the unauthorized use of hydrants. Canteens and the financial structures of most churches are designed to be conservative. Churches presume they hold limited resources, which will be difficult to obtain when the supply is exhausted. Churches whose financial structures resemble a fire hydrant know that the money is not inexhaustible, but they also know that money supports the outreach of the church. The financial structure of a healthy church, therefore, needs to be geared for distributing money to mission.

Keep these two images in mind as you think about money and mission:

1. Financial structure needs to be viewed in the context of the larger system. How money flows around a church is dependent upon the health of the entire organization. The whole budgeting process needs to be visible and open for input so that each church committee sees how the objectives they are trying to achieve fit in with the church's overall financial plan. When a congregation is in conflict, the usual sources of money dry up. If a church has low spiritual passion, its stewardship will be proportionately lower. In other words, people will give a smaller percentage of their income. If a church fails to empower people to take an active role in mission projects, then people will only give what is necessary to keep the roof from falling or to maintain the status quo. For this reason it is important for people who count and distribute church money not see themselves as bean counters, but as wise stewards. While being careful not to breach rules of confidentiality, the financial secretary of the church should ask why giving waxes and wanes. The finance committee should discuss what is happening in the community and how the lifestyle of the church membership affects their giving decisions. Is it, for example, time to enable credit card use in the church, or to offer members the option of giving through direct withdrawal from their bank account?

2. The financial structure must reinforce good stewardship and be culturally sensitive. Under the old paradigm (the norm before the "baby

boomer" generation entered church leadership positions), many churches built budgets upon a process that if someone demonstrated a need, showed prudent accountability, and told people what others had already committed to give, then people would give to support the budget. Today, people don't care what others are giving and they have no desire to support an institution for the sake of the institution. People want to know that what they give will make a difference. If giving adds meaning to our lives, we will give. Under the new paradigm, accountability is important (the audit still needs to be done), but missional impact is the heart of giving. The budget needs to be communicated as a series of ministries and objectives that people will fund to the extent their hearts, minds, and bodies are engaged with those plans.

Tithing

What about tithing? We need to stop speaking about tithing as the solution to all of our church problems. Consider this as a case where our "in house" language has leaked out into the congregation and is hurting our witness to those who are unchurched. We all know that if we could move our congregation from their current habit of giving three percent (or less) of their income to giving the biblical ten percent, we would meet all of the church's needs. A person who is not currently involved in church leadership, however, hears a self-serving, institution-over-people reasoning when they hear about tithing in this way. They say, "Tithing may work for you, but it doesn't work for me." Many people also view the concept of a biblical mandate with cynicism. Even many church leaders may privately think of tithing as an ancient law that is not appropriate or practical today. Or they think of tithing as a concept designed to make people feel guilty. Guilt is the kiss of death for any idea in today's culture.

We still need to talk about tithing. People today need to hear it in the context of their personal spiritual growth. We present the biblical goal of ten percent as a personal objective (like the goal of losing ten pounds) to which they can work to reach one step at a time. We say, "Tithing is how you loosen the grip that materialism has upon your life."

We set tithing within the context of the church's goal to transform the world. People get excited when they see that by tithing, their congregation will make a real difference in the lives of the homeless in their area and they will engage in a much larger ministry to offer hope to hopeless people. Tithing concerns restoring a generous heart to the people of God, which is more important than funding your current budget. Encourage people to give to the church's mission and to other groups that reach out around the world in love and mission.

Money to Missions

The two shifts mean we can no longer design and present our church budget as we always have. The purpose of the financial structure of the church is to direct money to missions. If the things supported by the church budget are not the things about which the community of faith feels passionate, then the budget needs radical change. If life-transforming ministries are not being empowered by the oversight of the church staff, then funding of certain staff positions may not be necessary. This shift in thinking can be coupled with the realization that lay staff and volunteers can lead, direct, and accomplish effective ministries rather than to hire additional clergy. Many large churches have moved towards hiring a number of part-time lay staff rather than someone to fill the traditional associate pastor. All people engage in ministry, a concept that Martin Luther described as the priesthood of all believers.

Many churches are finding that the best way to communicate the church's financial needs is to develop a "mission budget." The mission budget communicates the difference people are making through their giving. This budget is broken down into categories based upon the vital ministries and current short-term objectives of the church. It may have headings such as "Nurturing the People's Love of God through Worship" or "Reaching Out to the Neighborhood" or "The Goal for this Year: Expanding Parking." Overhead costs, such as building maintenance and pastoral staff, are proportioned to each category based upon the portion of that fixed cost the particular ministry uses. The mission budget also should include a list of specific items or percentage cuts/increases that will happen according to the pledges received or giving offered throughout the year. Support this understanding of giving with short "mission minutes" in worship. These short presentations tell how specific items have met human needs. People may also offer testimonies on how giving relates to our personal growth as disciples in Christ.

The congregation does not need to hear dour predictions about how much utilities are likely to rise in the coming year or how long it has been since we gave our pastor a decent raise. These "in house" concerns always lead people to say, "My gas bill has gone up too and I didn't get a raise this year." The factual expense compared to income form of the budget should still be presented, but on a separate page from the mission budget and with much less emphasis. Communicating how the money will get to the mission is the primary task of those who are working in the area of stewardship.

Limited Resources

What works well structurally in the long run relates to our core Christian values. One of the core values of our faith is generosity. By being generous, we proclaim that money is merely a tool, with little ultimate value in itself, to be used to accomplish good things. Jesus contrasted the joy of mission-driven people with the mindset of those who value institutional survival too highly. He spoke about the joy of the kingdom of God being like a pearl for which a man squandered everything to obtain (Matthew 13:44-46). In another, more challenging parable about money, Jesus spoke of the crooked accountant who used his master's money to buy friends for himself (Luke 16:1-9).

By way of contrast, the unstated motto of a finance committee may be "We don't have much to work with, so let's balance the budget and cut costs." This poverty mentality is in direct opposition to the gospel of abundant life. We need to concentrate on doing God's mission through our giving, and banish from our discussions the attitude which views cash as a limited resource.

Public Relations

The organizational structures that handle money in the church need to recognize that they have significant public relations functions. They must hold as their guiding principle the fact that Christians need to give in order to be healthy. Giving is a key step in discipleship formation and growth. The more intentional people are in giving money, the more likely that they are open to the power of God to transform their lives. At every step, the money to mission structure of the church needs to communicate and reinforce the transformative effect that giving has upon the giver.

Communicate intentionally at every step of the financial process:

- When receiving the offering in worship, offer scripture, prayer, and short "words about today's offering" to say that sacrificial giving is integral to worship.

- As the church council and mission committees disburse funds to projects, let the congregation know about the new relationships that are formed through their generosity. Mission reports and photographs from the field should be a regular part of the congregation's life.

- When the church focuses on its annual stewardship campaign, focus on the role giving plays in a person's spiritual formation.

Emphasize the "fire hydrant" thinking that goes with our missional vision rather than the wilderness canteen thinking of not having enough. Jesus proclaimed the abundant life as a new way of thinking of God's grace and love. Those of us who live in that grace will understand the ways that love transformed our lives.

CHAPTER SEVEN

Postscript: Build a New One or Fix the Old?

Mission first, People Always!

Military Saying

When Goliath showed up on that Palestinian plain long ago, he changed everything. Until that moment, the Philistines had been a nuisance. Each spring, Saul drafted an army and faced the Philistines. Goliath, however, posed a different kind of threat. He challenged Israel to a single "winner take all" battle. If Goliath won, the people of God would go into slavery (1 Samuel 17:9). If Goliath lost, then the Philistines would become slaves of Israel.

Congregations also face "do or die" situations. A fire or tornado might destroy their building. A furnace may fail or the roof may collapse, and the estimates for repair outstrip the congregation's resources. The crisis sometimes arises from a character flaw in their leadership. A member of the staff may be accused of sexual misconduct or some act of negligence may result in a lawsuit. Conflict may also step in like an uninvited giant and trample the unity of the congregation. Hindsight in these matters is always 20-20, and someone may point out how failure to follow certain procedures or practices created the crisis.

Notice how Saul and his army faced their hour of crisis. They hunkered down and did nothing. We sometimes see this same passivity in the church. Circumstances that propel some leaders to heroic efforts will cause others to retreat. After the fall of the roof or the schism within the church, one sees the remaining church leaders huddled in a defensive circle. There they may complain about inadequate support from their denomination or simply feel neglected; however, people do not respond apathetically to crisis because they lack empathy. Saul cared very much about the survival of his kingdom, but he and his officers no longer saw a connection between their success as a nation and the purposes of God. Goliath tested their missional vision, not their military preparedness. The same is true of every Goliath that shakes the walls of our congregations.

If a fire destroyed your church tonight, would you be able to build again? Would constructing a similar building in the same location be a wise thing? What do recent neighborhood trends tell you? Without its current structure, would your church lose its reason to exist? Is the sentimental feeling people have for this aging building the only thing that is keeping the congregation from merging with another nearby congregation? Now for the most difficult question: are you waiting for a crisis to take action?

I often hear the leadership of diminishing congregations speak about what they might do when the day finally comes that the church closes its doors. Their tone reminds me of the elderly person who knows that he or she can no longer live independently, but lacks the willingness (or the family support) to intentionally pick out an assisted living facility. As a pastor, I have noticed that people who proactively choose where they will live their final years remain active and engaged for a longer time. Those who wait until they break a hip or have some other crisis force them into a nursing home rarely seem as content with the choices others have made for them. As a church consultant, I am often called in to encourage church leaders as they develop a process to gracefully relocate or to downsize their facilities or to merge with another congregation. These congregations need leaders who will help them to pray, discern, and discover creative options before the giant shows up at their doorstep.

I sometimes wonder if Goliath's entry onto the field wasn't inevitable. The army of Saul had become institutional cowards. The nation was adrift under Saul's leadership and lacked a sustaining sense of purpose. The long narrative of the prophet Samuel ends as it began, "In those days the word of the LORD was rare; there were not many visions"(I Samuel 3:1b). In this weakened state, the nation would eventually be taken over by someone. Goliath provided a suitably sized, external villain—someone to blame other than Saul's leadership. Goliath also blessed Israel with a chance to rediscover their national identity and to move in a new direction. David's lucky shot did more than remove a giant; the victory gave the people a new vision of a heroic Israel.

The "what would you do if there was a fire" question is my way of discovering the pre-Goliath status of your congregation. Your church may be in a situation where having the opportunity to rebuild would be a blessing, because your ministries have outgrown your current structure. If you are typical of many mainline churches today, it is more likely that a fire would provide the opportunity to shed excess facility. We live in an era of declining worship attendance and a reduced need for program space. Compared with the boom era of the 1950s and church growth, most congregations are a pale shadow of their former glory. If a modern day Goliath, such as a fire, the sudden closure of a major employer, or the construction of a highway through your property were to step before your congregation, the crisis would bring into sharper focus the underlying status of your congregation's missional vision. If that vision no longer compels the people towards sacrificial courage, then it will take a miracle to overcome the structural problems that loom before you.

Choices

Like a car, you have only two choices as to what to do about your current structures. You can make modifications and do maintenance on your current model, or you can trade it in for something new. Unlike cars, new church structures do not come with a warranty or a listing in *Consumer's Reports* as to how satisfied other congregations are with similar structures. The fear of the unknown makes most church leaders favor gradual upgrades of existing structures over radical makeovers. New church buildings also cost significantly more than automobiles, and even when you amortize the cost of a new structure over many years, it remains a significant portion of the congregation's budget.

A further consideration is the fact that when you trade in your old clunker, you will lose some features that you may have enjoyed. The new car will not feel the same, and since its fenders aren't marked with three shades of primer, it may be harder for you to find in the mall parking lot. I still miss my sporty little '66 Toyota, even though it succumbed to terminal transmission problems in the midst of a cold Maine winter and forced me to walk everywhere for three months until I could buy another car. People will speak nostalgically about the "old church building" or the way "we used to do church council." Feelings of loss arise in every significant restructuring. These feeling must be accounted for and dealt with in a transitional process. The emotional trauma of demolition must be unpacked and ministered to, even if those who are leading the change wish to ignore it.

It is important to draw a clear distinction between maintenance activities and real restructuring. Often people will speak about minor rearrangements of church staff or about the remodeling of their sanctuary as if it is a major change. Church leaders also may be unrealistic about the benefits their changes will bring about. They expect a new coat of paint to do wonders for their sagging attendance. Frequent remodeling is an important part of wise building management. Even the best-run churches need to make constant modifications to their staffing and committee structure. This is not what I mean by radical restructuring. When buildings are restructured, something gets demolished. When organizations get restructured, jobs are restructured and relationships change. With this in mind I want to state three things:

- **Churches rarely significantly improve their effectiveness in evangelization or local missions without changing their structures.** Caterpillars cannot fly at all, no matter how much they want to or how passionately they envision it, until they undergo metamorphosis. Often a congregation will radically change how it is organized and this will improve their efforts at winning new people, which in turn, will propel the church to change its facility. Rarely, however, do outreach activities by themselves lead to church growth and transformation unless the church leaders are willing to embrace the need for structural change.

- **Radical restructuring must flow out of a renewed willingness to do mission or evangelization.** There is only one good reason for wanting to change the church: to make more disciples of Jesus Christ. Simply wanting to do something new doesn't offer any compelling reason to restructure. Wanting to bring new people into a relationship with God or wanting to serve the community provides sufficient spiritual motivation for undergoing the pain of radical change. Often a church will want to tear down an aging facility to save on energy costs. Unless there is a missional reason for their action, downsizing only staves off the inevitable closure of the church.

- **Restructuring is a transitional process and should be done in careful and prayerful steps.** Radical restructuring involves loss. Wise church leaders study the process of transition and seek to order the changes so that the congregation can adjust. They build listening into the change process. They ask, "What should we carry with us from the old over into the new?" They honor the contributions previous generations made to provide the edifice that is now being retired.

With these three principles in mind, I urge you never to sell a major restructuring as if it were a minor matter. Nor should one inflate minor remodeling projects into epic dramas. The decision-making center for routine adjustments to the church structure belongs in the appropriate committees. The congregation as a whole should not usurp the trust they have placed in their leadership by meddling in maters such as the color of a carpet or the details of a youth worker's expense account. In major restructuring, the decision-making center lies with the people. A congregation is making a statement about its spiritual identity when it changes its location or adopts a team-centered approach to pastoral ministry. Major restructuring is dependent upon visionary leaders. Those leaders, however, need to be the kind of mature individuals who patiently communicate until the tide shifts and the majority of the congregation is onboard with the change. Those leaders who guide their church through a significant change will discover that they have been making disciples in the process. The value of teaching others to reach further in their faith often exceeds the improvements won in the project.

Knowing this boundary is important because congregational conflict often arises when church leaders fail to manage the collective anxiety of the various parties affected by a change. The new building may already be paid for by a generous donation from a recent lottery winner, but there will still be complaints by those reared in the depression that the church cannot afford it. It is important to take the time to understand their feelings and to realize that people may be anxious for different reasons. There may be some who have qualms about the church using money tainted by gambling, others who wonder if it we shouldn't be doing more for missions and less for ourselves, and still others who question if there won't be some hidden costs to the project. Unpacking and addressing their concerns will be every bit as important as choosing the right architect or getting a good mortgage rate.

The Right Kind of Leadership

Good leaders never discount the human element of any decision. The military motto, "mission first, people always," applies particularly to those changes that bless a congregation with new structures. Any radical restructuring involves loss and dealing with that loss requires an intentional transitional process (see *The Church Transition Workbook*, Discipleship Resources). Even minor changes, however, require an awareness of how the affected structures fit into the church's overall mission. The good leader never loses sight of where the congregation is headed. If the stated objective of the congregation is to double its size in five years, then the sacrifices made today for expanded parking space make sense even if the lot is rarely full. The good leader, however, is also aware that this makes no sense at all to the person who has not fully appropriated the objective of growing the church. So when an elderly gentleman complains about all the money the church is spending to purchase and tear down adjacent homes, the wise leader does not discount him as an "old fogy." She considers again how to communicate the objectives of the church. She reminds herself that while the mission must come first, people always matter.

In fact, that is the real lesson of this book: Structures are by definition inanimate and unfeeling things, but they must serve human need. Any structure that does not function for the good of people must be changed. As we change structures, however, we always must be aware of how people feel about those structures. In the end, it will not be reason and logical precision that will matter most for this task; it will be faith, hope, and the constant application of love.

May the God who guided David against Goliath guide your journey.

Other Books by Bill Kemp

Each of the six books of this series will focus on problems that can become woven into a congregation's very culture, and so need the coordinated work of many people to achieve change. The emphasis is upon cultivating a broad leadership base that is aware of the issues and of implementing systemic changes. These books provide a common language that both laity and clergy can use together when they talk about the things that influence the success of their congregation.

- *Ezekiel's Bones* reveals how spiritual passion is the fuel that keeps a congregation active and excited about the faith it has to share with the world. Without spiritual passion, a church, no matter its size, will either crash and burn or become a hollow shell of its former glory. Just as the body is fueled by a nutritious diet, so a church is fueled by a healthy, passionate, spirituality.

- *Peter's Boat* looks at a common condition in today's world: burnout. Burnout threatens our relationships and our ability to function, especially as disciples of Jesus Christ. For everyone in the church, this book identifies the factors that lead to burnout and offers solutions to perfectionism, negative self-image, work addition, and overload.

- *Jonah's Whale* discusses how to keep the congregation united behind a common vision. How do we get to where we are going unless we know where it is and what path we should take towards it?

- *David's Harp* deals with preventing, managing, and transitioning out of conflict. Every pilot must communicate and respond to negative information in order avoid stormy weather and collisions with other planes. We tend to treat conflict as an unwelcome intruder, rather than a routine part of flying. This book helps church leaders not to panic, but to see God's purposes in stressful situations.

- *Jesus' New Command* deals with how to unite the congregation into a strong faith community. Love is like oxygen, vital to the maintenance of church life. This book provides tools for building intimate small groups while encouraging the congregation to be welcoming to newcomers.

Holy Places, Small Spaces (Discipleship Resources, 2005) looks at how small-church fellowships are faring compared to other congregations. It addresses the critical clergy supply problem and charts the changes that must take place for there to be a hopeful future of survival and growth for these congregations.

The Church Transition Workbook (Discipleship Resources, 2004) describes a step-by-step process that will enable the church to get moving again after traumatic conflict or being "run over by change." It keeps laity and clergy on the same page, as the church redefines pastoral relationships. The book includes stories, practical tools, and activities that will help the church see its current reality and the possibilities for ministry.